Off Grid Living

How to Plan and Execute Living off the Grid

(Shelter, Water, Energy, Heat, and More)

By: Barton Press

Copyright © 2020 by Barton Press

ALL RIGHTS RESERVED

No part of this book may be reproduced, stored in a retrieval system, or transmitted in any form or by any means, electronic, mechanical, photocopying, recording, scanning, or otherwise, without the prior written permission of the publisher.

Limit of Liability/Disclaimer of Warranty: the publisher and the author make no representations or warranties with respect to the accuracy or completeness of the contents of this work and specifically disclaim all warranties, including without limitation warranties of fitness for a particular purpose. No warranty may be created or extended by sales or promotional materials. The advice and strategies contained herein may not be suitable for every situation. This work is sold with the understanding that the publisher is not engaged in rendering medical, legal or other professional advice or services. If professional assistance is required, the services of a competent professional person should be sought. Neither the publisher nor the author shall be liable for damages arising herefrom. The fact that an individual, organization or website is referred to in this work as a citation and/or potential source of further information does not mean that the author or the publisher endorses the information the individuals, organization or website may provide or recommendations they/it may make. Further, readers should be aware that websites listed on this work may have changed or disappeared between when this work was written and when it is read.

Table of Contents

Introduction 1
    What We Know 2
    The Popularity of Off-Grid Living 7

PART ONE: Planning 10

CHAPTER 1: PUTTING THE IDEA IN WRITING 10
    TABLE 1 11
    The Rough Sketch 12
    Do Not Rush to Purchase Floor Plans 14

CHAPTER 2: Back of the Napkin Math - Does it Make Sense? 15
    Cost of the Land 16
    Square Footage of Building 17
    Power Generation 18
        Solar Power 18
        Wind Power 19
    Administrative Costs 20
    Total the Big-Ticket Items 21

CHAPTER 3 - Finalizing the Playbook by Putting Together the Running Task List 22
    TABLE 2 24

PART TWO - Execution 27

CHAPTER 4 - Get That Money Down! Cash or Financing? 27
    Interest Rates 27

Down Payment 28

Bank Locally? Or With a Chain? 29

Preparing for Initial Bank Meeting 30

The Pre-Commitment Process 31

What Closing Costs Mean 32

What is Title Insurance and Why am I Required to Pay for it? 33

CHAPTER 5 - Getting Legal: Permits: Deeds, Rights of Way, and Contracts 35

The Purchase and Sale Contract 35

Seeking Permission to Build 38

Building Permit 38

The Hearing Before the Local Commission 39

Do I come with an Attorney? 40

Wastewater Permit 41

What is a Wastewater Permit? 41

Understand your Home State's Regulations Before Consulting with an Attorney 42

Understanding the Deed - Devil in the Details 42

The Warranty Deed - the Gold Standard in Property Transfers 43

The Quitclaim Deeds - Buyers Beware! 44

Administrator or Executor's Deed 45

Rights-of-Way Define Who Else Can Access the Property 45

PART THREE: Building 47

CHAPTER 6: Construction - What Can You Do to Maximize Efficiency? 47

Find a Builder Who Will Also Act as a Teacher 48

Timber.. 50

Straw Bale Homes 51

Cob/Wattle and Daub 52

Stone 54

    Recycled materials 55

Shipping Containers 55

Types of Homes on Wheels... 58

    Campers 58

    Trailers 58

    Conversions 59

CHAPTER 7: The Pros and Cons of a Tiny House 61

Financing 63

Adapting to Smaller Spaces 64

Storage 64

Taxes and Living Expenses. Are Tiny Homes Cheaper? 65

Property Taxes 66

Water, Sewer, and Electricity... 66

Heating and cooling 67

Groceries 68

Laundry.. 68

Appliances 69

PART FOUR - Completion 71

CHAPTER 8 - Water Supply 71

Step One - Determine Your Water Requirements 71

- Rainfall 72
- Low-Flow Appliances 73
- Change You Usage Habits 73

Choosing the Right Water Supply 75

- Natural Spring 75
- Test Before You Consider 76
- Do You Need a Water Filtration System? 76
- Where is the Spring Located? 77
- Installing the Water Line 77
- How Deep Does the Water Line Need to Be? 78

Well 79

CHAPTER 9: The Bathroom - Where and What You Need 81

A Discussion About Outhouses 81

- Blow the Stench Away 82
- Down the Hill 82
- The Outhouse Does Not Need to be Ugly 82
- Water Hookup? 83

Composting Toilet 83

- Systemic composting 84
- Self-composting toilet 84
- Composting Toilets Do Not Need to Be Outhouses 84

Conventional Toilet 86

    Low flow 86

Shower, Tub or Both? 87

    Why a Shower Stall Makes Sense 87

    Outdoor Showers 88

    The Permanent Outdoor Shower 89

    Camping/Portable Outdoor Showers 89

    Saving Water with a Bathtub 90

    Completing the Water Saving Project with the Right Sink 90

    Small is Best 91

    Wall-Mounted Sink 91

    Vessel Above-Counter Sink 91

    Corner Wall Mounted Sink 92

CHAPTER 10: Deciding on a Power System 93

First-Weigh the Cost Versus the Incentives 93

What Programs Exist to Reduce the Cost? 93

Tax Credits 94

State Tax Incentives/Rebates 94

Local/Municipal Incentives 95

Solar 95

    Do I Cut Tree Down or Remove Limbs? 98

    Does the Ground Need to Be Modified to Capture More Sun? 99

Wind 100

    What Role Do I Want Wind Power to Play in Power Generation? 102

    Matching Cost with Power Output 102

Determining Benefits Versus Negatives 103

What About Zoning Regulations? 103

Wind Feasibility Study 104

Size of Turbine 105

Is the Site Really Worth It? 106

CHAPTER 11: Heat Sources - Options 108

Wood Heat - The Age-Old Classic 108

Finding the Source 109

Do It Yourself? Are You Sure You Can? 109

What wood are you cutting? 109

How much wood do you need? 110

How quickly can I burn wood that has been cut? 110

After You Have Committed to Wood, Choose a Stove 110

Stove Choices 111

Open Fireplace 112

Potbelly Stove 112

Traditional Cookstove 113

Masonry Stove 114

Modern Day Woodstove 114

Wood Pellet Stoves 115

Now the Negative 116

Never Stop Looking to Close Up Outdoor Leaks 117

Geothermal Heating and Cooling 117

Take note! 117

Vertical closed-loop systems 118

  Horizontal closed-loop systems 118

  Open-loop systems 118

Chapter 12: Putting It All Together 120

Introduction

Barry was a Vietnam veteran who had come home after fighting for his country and wanted to get away from it all. After moving back to central Vermont, he and his wife, Martha, found 30 acres of land located in the heart of the Vermont Green Mountains. The land, which was a mixture of forest and rundown pastures, was serviced by a winding dirt road that was a little more than a glorified four-wheeler trail.

Just five years prior, the local power company had offered to build power lines to service the farms located on the mountain. The largest landowner, a small-scale cow farmer, declined, questioning why he needed to be indebted to someone else when he could provide the necessities he and his family needed with his own two hands.

The barn for Martha and Barry came first. It was a necessity, as it would house their chickens and goats. They were to be a primary food source for the first year. The cabin came next, a 1000 square foot 3-bedroom home with a self-composting toilet and a trickle of running water that fed the kitchen sink. There was no blender, no microwave, and no television. They lived with only a battery-powered radio that could pick up three local stations to serve as the nighttime entertainment for them each evening after work and chores.

For the early years, Martha and Barry's off-grid home was functional and nothing more. It was not easy; it took a great deal of commitment. There were times they wondered if they had made the right decision because it was not an easy life. In the end, it was the peace, privacy, and feelings of self-sufficiency that were their reward.

For Martha and Barry, their Green Mountain log cabin started a 30-year story of living off-grid. In that home, they raised six children, built three additions to their home, harvested thousands of board feet of timber, and drank gallons of fresh goat milk.

Their off-grid home represented more than a place to rest their heads - it was a symbol of how they wished to live their lives; to model, for their children, and it served as an example of what self-sustenance was. They hoped to instill these basic tenets of living life to its fullest if their children would like to grow up and continue the tradition.

The idea of living off-grid can sound like a romantic utopia. Frankly, if you are looking for a comfortable life with plenty of idle time, then living off-grid may not be for you. However, for those who are interested in a self-sustained, enriching experience where you are less reliant on others and more independent, providing for yourself and your family, living off-grid is an excellent choice to help lead you to this goal.

What We Know

The basic premise of living off-grid is to construct a residence free of any reliance on a utility company for generating its power. As has been well documented, the mass production of energy has fueled growing concerns regarding the fossil fuels burned to generate such power.

The carbon emissions from these power generators are a major component in the rapidly evolving global climate change crisis that has taken center stage for most countries as they grapple with rising sea levels and increasingly unpredictable and severe weather patterns. In 2020, during the writing of this book, we surpassed the entire alphabet and began using Greek alphabet for names of hurricanes and tropical storms in the Atlantic and Gulf of Mexico.

The Pacific Northwest of the United States is on fire again, and the map overview looks like an inferno as five states burn out of control. This is also a climate issue that can be directly blamed on global warming, which is a result of burning fossil fuels and releasing carbon emissions into our atmosphere.

As further motivation for enacting change to our current way of life, the recent public health crisis brought on by COVID-19, has provided additional incentive as it continues to reveal national infrastructure vulnerabilities.

As deliveries were slowed, most of the United States experienced shortages of food items and dry goods. Toilet paper became a commodity that was hoarded, and would-be profiteers attempted to sell Americans a single roll of toilet paper for as much as $40 on sites like Amazon and eBay. Fines were levied, and arrests were made in some cases, such as when a man was found to have a garage full of hand sanitizer.

Brothers, Matt and Noah Calvin, drove around their local area in Tennessee and hoarded hand sanitizer and other sanitation supplies that people were seeking during the pandemic.

After stockpiling over 17,000 bottles of hand sanitizer in a garage, they began selling bottles of dollar store hand sanitizer for as much as $70 per bottle on the internet. Desperate people were paying the prices out of fear.

Ultimately, the men were shut down and charged with price gouging, but it is a prime example of how the world can be turned on end when you least expect it. Those who were desperate were victims. Many have had their eyes opened very wide during these times of living in an epidemic.

In response to the rising level of concern, individuals and families have begun to look for ways to separate themselves from the chaos. Even more people believe that we could see issues with the national power grids.

These grids have not only placed an increased strain on the earth but also have created a higher risk of widespread power failure. As people turn the air conditioning down in summer and heat up during winter, the power grids are pushed to the point of rolling brown-outs, and total black-outs in some areas.

There is no better example of the volatility of the national power grid than Hurricane Sandy, which caused power outages to 8.1 million homes along the east coast in 2012. Even more recently, in 2016, Hurricane Harvey dumped more than 40 inches of rain on the Houston, Texas area. Thirty-thousand Americans were displaced, and more than 17,000 rescues were necessary after Harvey hit Texas and 336,000 people in Texas were left without power.

This power outage crippled millions of people trying to perform their daily routines and resulted in billions of dollars in damages and weeks of outages while ensuring that power was back up and running.

While this band-aide has temporarily fixed the immediate issue, it has in no way solved it. Instead, what remains is the same infrastructure as before, which is just as susceptible to failure. The risk of natural disasters continues to rise due to climate change, leaving us in the classic catch-22 of relying on a system that continues to put us at increased risk.

Some of the most hardcore off-grid residents have chosen to combat the grid dilemma by creating homes that have no power at all. Historically for generations, families made-do with kerosene lights and wood fireplaces; some families still live this way today.

When Barry and Martha moved to their log cabin in central Vermont, for the first two years, they relied solely on fire energy. It was hard, so eventually they turned to a small solar panel and a generator for supplemental power use in the mid-1990s. For the sake of survival, it met their needs.

There remain some people that are fully committed to living with no power. A settlement outside Albuquerque, New Mexico is home to over 300 citizens who elected to purchase cheap land with no access to any public utilities, such as running water and electricity.

These people are called 'preppers' because they are prepping for a time when the grid could go down permanently. They believe that it is inevitable that we'll lose the power grid entirely, whether it be from sabotage of a foreign influencer's doing or a major catastrophic weather event.

Some preppers are 'end of timers' who believe in the resurrection and that the planet will be in the 'end of days,' which will result in total devastation. Others will come to steal your things because the infrastructure will completely fall apart. Humans and animals will starve, and only those who have hoarded supplies and prepared will survive this apocalypse.

Others have come to believe that anything is possible, and we should simply be prepared. The pandemic in 2020 has solidified this desire to be prepared for anything. If 2020 has taught us anything, it surely is that those who are prepared will not have to fight over a package of toilet paper when the day of shortage arrives. The off-grid preppers have barely blinked at all over our chaos and uncertainty.

More Americans are beginning to think that living off-grid and being more prepared for any situation is the way to live. Living off-grid means you are nearly unaffected by the chaos of the world around you. Can you imagine how wonderful your life could be without a commute each morning and not needing to go to the grocery store or pay another electric bill as long as you live?

For those who wish to live the most natural off-grid lifestyle, the planning and building of the home might be a little less complex. Instead of focusing on the right power generation from natural resources, the focus will center on the construction of the home. This cuts down on the usefulness of this book, but it requires a lot of the same planning because the requirements for construction remain the same.

It is clear, however, that a majority of people who have committed to off-gridliving do not wish to abstain fully from electric power in finding a suitable way to fuel their homes. Most are simply seeking to buck the national trend, be more environmentally conscious, and wish to bring a level of self-reliance that will survive the unpredictable variations and risks that come with being hooked to a national power grid.

There is also the consideration that you may live very cheaply when there are no utility bills coming to your mailbox every month that threaten to cut you off from the things you use in your daily lives. Electricity and water can both be harvested and used, completely free from monthly obligations.

The Popularity of Off-Grid Living

The interest in off-grid living has exploded in the last 10 years. New data from the International Renewable Energy Agency (IRENA) has reported that 115 million people globally depend on solar for generating power. Another 25 million have utilized solar to create their mini-grid to generate all of their power. Additionally, some 6 million people have used hydropower as their main electric source. There are also other methods of harnessing energy, and we'll cover those, so continue reading.

What was in recent history identified as an alternative lifestyle, the evolution of the alternative energy market has made off-grid living much more obtainable to a wider range of people. According to a study conducted by IRENA, Solar PV module prices have fallen by around 80% since the end of 2009, while wind turbine prices have fallen by 30–40%.

The dramatic drop in cost for solar and wind, have increased the overall consumer demand for these products, which in turn has fueled numerous startup companies who are looking to capitalize on this rising trend by offering financing and installation of power systems to consumers.

What the rising interest in natural and localized power generation has shown is that there is an increased drive by the global community to change how power is generated, which in turn will provide further independence to control more aspects of their lives.

There has also been a relatively new market opening in recent years. Solar panels that were some of the earlier installations have begun to wear out and need to be replaced. These used panels are being recycled by after some necessary upgrades and being sold as used for discounted prices. This is opening a market for DIY projects, allowing some people to gain access to entry-level prices with bigger panels that have traditionally been exclusively installed by contractors.

The purpose of this book is to provide the reader with three major takeaways:

1. To spark interest in off-the-grid living.

2. To stimulate contemplation of how off-grid living can be accomplished.

3. To motivate you with the keys to put your plan into action.

Each reader needs to seek independent professional advice on the planning and building process. Living off-grid is not a cookie-cutter process. Indeed, it is meant to be quite the opposite of that. It is filled with unique scenarios that will need to be independently reviewed and planned for. It is a way of life that allows you to weave your own creativeness into your home and the way you live.

Living off-grid is a challenge that can allow you to unleash your ingenuity and learn new ways of doing things that integrate modern twists on the old ways of doing things. It is a combination of the old ways of doing things with the technology that we've come to learn from.

Many new off-grid homes are in a hybrid style that incorporates many of the old ways, with modern twists that make off-grid homes into works of art that are mind-bogglingly superior in how they can use sunlight and passive heating and cooling with such efficiency.

Despite the disclaimer, off-grid living's primary requirements are motivation and initiative. Although the task of creating an off-grid home may be daunting at first, seeing through the trees to an ultimate goal can fuel endless opportunity.

As with any opportunity, the first step in capturing it is to take the proverbial first step out the door. As you continue to take each additional step, the picture will be clearer and more obtainable.

PART ONE: Planning

CHAPTER 1: PUTTING THE IDEA IN WRITING

Great ideas can come from a wide range of inspiration. To find this inspiration, you must first wade through many irrelevant thoughts. By wading through the good and the bad, you will, through utter determination, reach the ideas that yield the highest chance of being productive. There is no greater way to start the inspirational process than to commit your thoughts to paper.

This brainstorming will not be organized at first. Instead, it will come in more of a stream of consciousness that you can spew out onto the paper. It doesn't need to be pretty at this stage. Just get it out on paper.

It is important at this stage not to be self-conscious about what you write. It may be nearly illegible, poetic, or complete nonsense. It may be in drawings -- whatever makes sense to you.

The only important thing is that you keep writing it. Sooner or later, ideas will emerge from the chicken scratch that will rise to the top of your brain as you digest your initial thoughts on off-grid living.

After you have sifted through enough words to fill an entire notebook page, circle back, and grab a highlighter to mark the relevant ideas for your off-grid project. Then, be sure to put these onto a separate sheet of paper or type them into a chart on your computer. They may simply be keywords, research ideas, or trade names of materials you have used before.

After you have completed the initial transfer of ideas, continue the stream of thoughts by continuing the process of documenting all your thoughts on paper. After you have started to create the keywords, your rambling will become more concise, and each subsequent page, after the first, will generate an increased number of keywords.

After you feel you have written enough, it is then time to take your highlights and organize them into categories. An example of this charting could look something like this:

TABLE 1

Planning	Land	Home	Power
Permits required	Need more than 1 acre	1,000, 2,000, or 3,000 sq feet?	Solar, Wind…Geo-Thermal?
Organizational professionals? Who to hire and when?	Mountains? Fields? Where is the best for power exposure	How do you maximize efficiency?	Local companies, are they worth it?
Ballpark costs to retain experts.	The money is the key	Bank financing? Private financing?	Do they finance?

As you can see, these ideas are not fully developed; they are simply placed into categories to allow you to develop them further as your thoughts become clearer.

The Rough Sketch

Beyond describing the type of off-grid home you wish to build in words, it is also important to start putting these ideas into the form of a rough sketch. Sketching a floor plan or layout of the property will allow you to begin analyzing the feasibility of your idea. By reducing an idea into a drawing, you have begun to bring the idea to life. Putting anything onto paper changes it from a dream to a goal. You've created a mission with an action plan.

There is a wide range of floor plan drawing applications that can be found online. Programs such as Smartdraw offer a free 7-day trial and are very user friendly. Although the technology available is seemingly endless, in the early sketching process, there is no substitute for the graph paper and pencil. You may have some great ideas but also remember that when you find your property, some of your sketches will change with the lay of the land, the terrain, and water that is or isn't on the property.

Using your hands to create on paper instead of typing buttons on your computer or dragging your mouse on a desk will stimulate further ideas. It has been extensively studied that putting pencil to paper stimulates a different cognitive process than typing. This especially applies to generating creative ideas, such as a rough sketch of your future off-grid home.

Keep in mind that this sketch does not have to be exact; it does not even need to have straight lines. It is a continuation of the thought stimulation process that will help you open up and think outside of the box you've been in until now. By connecting your stream of consciousness with a sketch, you are starting to piece together a cognizant idea that you can then begin to break down into obtainable steps.

After coming up with a sketch and a narrative, you can further enhance your planning by seeking the inspiration of others. A good start is to search for off-grid images that may catch your eye and provide you with ideas that you had not thought of before. Pinterest is a perfect way to find photos of fencing ideas, cabin ideas, water collection ideas, and so much more.

A prime example of inspiration searching is the shipping container off-grid home. Many, including this author, had not even considered a shipping container to be an acceptable idea for an off-grid home until a few photos emerged during an internet search. When looking at some of the designs and what these homes look like as finished products, it became easy to see why a shipping container might make sense for some off-grid homeowners.

The shipping container is just one of many examples of why it is important to research the farthest corners of design ideas early in the process. Going through this process expands your thinking, opens your mind to new possibilities, and allows you to continue your thought process.

Remember, it is not the quality of ideas at this early stage; it is the quantity. As with most brainstorming, there is strength in the number of ideas you can reduce to writing. At this point, it doesn't matter how many ideas turn out to be viable. It is more important to simply keep the momentum going than to evaluate feasibility in this early stage. Simply put, keep writing, no matter what product comes out. You can evaluate the fruits of your thought processes later.

Do Not Rush to Purchase Floor Plans

Many who are interested in an off-grid home will commit financial resources too early in the process. At the information spewing part of your planning, building plans are a waste of money.

These plans provide way too much detail. By committing money, you are running the risk of being boxed into an idea before you have fully vetted it. This premature action will only limit the creative process, which may block great ideas from coming to the surface.

Utilize other free ideas, but do not spend money unnecessarily. Once you have completed further research and have come to a solid plan, you can always circle back to building plans to see if they still fit your goals and are now worth the investment.

The odds are in your favor that you won't need the plans, and you'll be better off to wait until you are standing on your property, investigating the lay of the land, the slope, and where the sun moves across the sky from sunrise to sunset.

In fact, I strongly encourage you not to place your solar panels permanently until you've lived through all four seasons and determined where your panels will get optimum sunlight during all four seasons. The position of the sun changes, and having panels that can be positioned differently is a huge positive step. Mounting them on a roof is not always the best choice, so don't make assumptions about such things until you are firm with feet on terra firma.

CHAPTER 2: Back of the Napkin Math - Does it Make Sense?

Now that you have begun to formulate an idea for your off-grid home, the next step in the process is to start the calculation process on what the project will cost. Keep in mind that this early calculation is not meant to be a formal budget; it is intended to merely be a ballpark. You should know what your budget is and how to stay within that budget. In this chapter, we'll show you what to do to keep your project on point.

One important aspect of ballpark math is to round your calculations up by adding %10% to your estimate as a variable fee. There are always expenses that you cannot foresee in the planning process. Instead of guessing at what these variables will be, add 10%% to each rough estimate. This will allow you to further enhance your ballpark figure while not going too deep into detail.

Remember, costs are not cemented at this time. They are only meant to stimulate further motivation in the planning process when it becomes clear by your rough math that the project may be feasible.

It will open your mind to what you are capable of and what is completely out of reach. When it comes to off-grid living, there are homes for all budgets, including tiny pallet homes entirely built from free pallet wood. Free pallets can be used for counters, wall covering, and much more.

It is always better to overestimate and be pleasantly surprised when the cost to build your home is lower, rather than be surprised at the cost, which could mean you do not have enough money to complete the project. You can always use the savings to put toward another pet project on your homesteads, such as gardens, chicken coops, or goat sheds.

We will go through the back of the napkin math using a standard 2000 square foot, 3 bed, and 2-bathroom home. This example will give you a baseline that you can easily adjust to fit your roughly sketched outline. This scenario is just another step in the conceptualization process. We are simply taking one small step forward in gathering ideas by applying numbers to our rough sketches.

Cost of the Land

As the old market analogy goes, real estate is all about location. When it comes to off-grid living, the value of the land is all about its exposure to the natural resources that will make up its power generation. A running water source can supply you with generated hydropower and provide you with a source of water at the same time. That property is worth more than a desert plot with no water and little rainfall. This explains why an acre in the California desert is $300, and an acre in the lush green areas across the mid-west are several thousand dollars.

It is impossible to know exactly what the cost of land will be at this stage in the calculation. However, it is easy enough to find the cost of land that is currently on the market that may be in the area which you desire for your home.

Again, you're looking for a ballpark figure. A quick look at Realtor.com or Zillow will allow you to break down your searches into location, cost, and acreage. A little more research, and you'll be able to get a rough estimate of what land is selling per acre on average.

For our example, we searched parcels ranging between 5 and 10 acres that have been listed for sale in two southern Vermont counties. The average cost for vacant land was between $5,000 and $10,000 per acre. For our back of the napkin math, we used $7,500 per acre and multiplied it by 7.5 acres, a modest but certainly usable acreage for an off-the-grid home.

Cost of Land: $7,500 x 7.5 acres = $56,250 + 10%% variable fee = $61,875.

Now you have a general budget for the land that you're looking for. You've got a list of things written down that should help you with a checklist to determine which property hits all your desires and dreams for your off-grid hideaway.

Square Footage of Building

For our example, we calculate that the house is going to be built, not purchased. It is certainly a possibility for an existing home to be converted into an off-the-grid home.

However, since there are so many variables that go into purchasing an existing home -- such as the condition of the electric power, the home's location, and how close it is located to the existing power grid -- that would cause our already rough estimates to be even tougher.

Square footage of the living space of your home is one of the easiest ways to calculate the cost to build it. Depending on the quality of materials and the design, the cost to build the home will range between $100 and $155 per square foot.

Again, don't be discouraged if this seems too high for your personal budget. Remember that depending on the type and size of the home, you can save a lot on materials by recycling and upcycling building materials.

If you plan on building a 2,000 square foot home, you should plan for at least $200,000 and upwards of $310,000 for the construction costs alone. For our example, we used the middle of the road cost per square foot of $125.

Ballpark Cost for Construction of Home: $250,000 + 10%% variable fee = $275,000

Power Generation

The first step in estimating the cost to install a power generation system is to determine precisely how much energy you will need monthly. The energy usage is largely tied to the size of the home as well as the number of occupants. A general estimate for our 2,000 square foot home is that it will require 1,000 kWh per month.

Calculating the cost of power generation is where costs can be wildly miscalculated. At this point in the planning, you likely have a rough idea as to what type of electrical system you want. It is also likely that you will be able to roughly articulate the type of heating system that is desirable. You will be able to get into the details later, but for the rough math, here are a couple of estimates that can put you in the ballpark.

Solar Power

There is no better tool for initial research on the cost of a solar system for your home than the solar estimator located at https://news.energysage.com. This tool allows you to receive estimates for solar systems that are geared towards your exact location.

Although there is no substitute for contacting solar installation companies directly and receiving a quote, you are not at that stage yet with your back of the napkin math. Thus, this tool will suffice for the initial math.

For our example, we will calculate the cost based on an estimate generated for southern Vermont, and we will use the higher end of the tool to generate our back of the napkin math. Continuing with an estimate for a 2,000 square foot house, a rough cost for the system needed would be 10 kWh.

This ballparks the cost for the solar power system at $24,000 + 10%%variable fee = $26,400.

Wind Power

It is harder to find an accurate tool for generating estimates for wind-generated systems. The best estimate for wind is based on per kilowatt-hour produced. Rough estimates show that the cost per kWh is between $3,000 and $8,000.

For a large house, the desired output of electricity is 10 kWh, which on the high end equates to an $80,000 investment in power generation. For our example of a 2,000 square foot home, we will use the middle of the road estimate of $60,000 + 10%%variable fee = $66,000 for a fully installed system.

Geothermal

It should be noted that, before making any geothermal calculations, it is not as commonly available when compared to solar and wind power.

Before getting too far into the math for a potential geothermal power system, you should first research some of the frequently asked questions about the availability of these systems by visiting the Department of Energy (https://www.energy.gov) to ensure that geothermal is available in your area.

This initial research will either eliminate the idea of geothermal or will allow you to take the next step in researching its viability for your project. Regardless, you will have saved a lot of time by answering these questions early in the process.

Although geothermal energy production is not as well-known as wind and solar power, mostly due to its limited availability, it can be a practical off-grid energy source in certain areas. The best estimate for creating a localized geothermal power generating plant is $2,500 per installed kWh.

Using our example for the 8 kWh system that we calculated for solar and wind, the ballpark cost to install a geothermal system would be $20,000 + 10% variable fee = $22,000.

Administrative Costs

One of the least planned for costs in building an off-grid home, is the administrative costs required to receive permits and the closing costs on any bank financing. The details of these costs will be discussed further within this text.

For this exercise, however, it is safe to assume that it should be budgeted that administrative costs will fall in the ballpark of $7,500 with again a 10% markup allowing for the final cost.

Administrative Costs: $7,500 + 10% variable fee = $8,250

Total the Big-Ticket Items

Now that you have calculated the big-ticket items, you'll need to add the totals up to give yourself a running total for the project cost.

With the variables in energy production, we will see that in our 2,000 square foot home concept, the cost to build the home and to install an off-grid electrical service would come with a rough price tag of:

Solar: $366,425

Wind: $405,625

Geothermal: $361,625

Once the rough numbers have been run, the off-grid vision becomes clearer. If you are fortunate enough to have the ballpark amount of cash handy, you are a few steps ahead.

However, for most people, the costs merely give them further tasks to complete regarding the availability of financing. At least now, with some numbers to work with, the tasks are getting simpler and the target is far closer to achieving them. You can begin to see things happening now.

CHAPTER 3 - Finalizing the Playbook by Putting Together the Running Task List

Now that you have brainstormed and performed some rough calculations, it is time to put some detail into your planning by constructing a modifiable checklist, also known as the running task list. This will be your game plan. It can be modified as necessary, but it will be your guide to ensure that you've taken care of all the details.

It is at this point in the process where your ideas begin to take shape, and you can further develop your ideas by adding comprehensive concepts to what were generalizations beforehand. You can begin thinking about the way your kitchen will look, the type of walls you'll be installing, and what color your paint will be. Your vision is taking shape, and you're on a path that is clearly before you and on paper.

To begin construction of the running task list, you need to have in front of you; the refined stream of consciousness or chart of keywords, your rough calculations, your rough sketch of your home, and access to the internet.

Sit down at a table and begin to break down your notes into achievable steps. As simple as it seems, your #1 task on the list, should be to make this list itself. Writing down the task gets the ball rolling and, while you are applying your hand to paper, your brain will start to conceptualize the task in front of you, which will further your progress.

While coming up with tasks, be as concise as possible. If you need to contact your local bank to inquire about financing, be sure to put the bank and the phone number on the list.

When you go back to this list to execute the tasks, getting the details you need to cross it off your list can make it easier to perform while still battling the temptation to come up with an excuse not to take action now (such as not having a handy number).

The best way to ensure your list is completed timely, is to not only make it easy to access the information, but also to give yourself reasonable deadlines to complete each task. Don't think you should perform a huge number of tasks every day.

Give yourself reasonable space in between deadlines to ensure that you take the time needed to fully complete one task before moving on to another. It will be better to take the proper time to do these things so that all is done properly.

It is also important to develop your task list in chronological order: the lower the number, the more immediate the task. By constructing the task list in chronological order, you are not only organizing your thoughts, but you are also building the instruction manual for completion. By adhering to a step-by-step process that follows a specific timeline, you are making the tasks that much easier to complete.

Sit down and take your time; the list does not need to be completed all in one day. Give yourself a reasonable amount of time each day but make sure that it is solely dedicated to developing the list. You might also wish to use a pencil so that you can make changes and erase some things as you work on the details and prioritization of tasks.

Do not allow yourself to be distracted by other things while you are constructing your list. Limiting the risk of outside interference will ensure that whatever time you have allotted for the generation of your tasks will be productive. It is not about the amount of time that you dedicate to the process, but the efficiency in which you utilize that time.

For our 2,000 square foot example, the beginning of a good running task list may look something along the following lines:

TABLE 2

5	Task	Deadline	Notes
1	Construct a running task list	5/15/2020	
2	Call bank to inquire about financing - Bob, bank manager 802-257-1133	5/15/2020	
3	Complete mortgage application.	5/25/2020	
4	Schedule meeting with a contractor for building- Peter at Klien Builders. 802-767-4431	6/1/2020	
5	Research the best locations for solar and wind generation, are there any maps to show the best areas? Contact Efficiency Vermont (802-885-1478) to begin the research process.	6/5/2020	

6	Is Geo-Thermal an option for power generation? Call VT Agency of Energy 802-885-0056	6/10/2020	
7	Meet with the realtor (Sarah 802-777-9834) regarding vacant land for sale.	6/15/2020	
8	Get 3 quotes for energy production: Catamount Solar-802-257-8761 King's Wind Generation: 603-999-7676 Geo-Thermal?	6/30/2020	
9	Follow up with the Bank to ensure mortgage application is processing. Bob, bank manager 802-257-1133	7/5/2020	
10	Find 3 plots of land that meet energy production needs.	8/1/2020	
11	Consult with an attorney (Sam: 802-275-4327) to inquire about how to make an offer on land.	8/15/2020	
12	Meet with Klein Construction to visit prospective land purchases	8/25/2020	

13	Schedule site visits with solar, wind, and Geo-Thermal (if feasible) on potential land purchases.	9/1/2020	
14	Make Offer on land	9/10/2020	
15	Close land deal	10/1/2020	
16	Break Ground and begin construction.	11/1/2020	

The above running task list is in no way a fully comprehensive list. There will likely be other tasks that come up along the way that will change the deadlines. Embrace this change as it will ensure that you are continuing the brainstorming process and further refining your ideas to ensure that you are completing each task as thoroughly as possible before you move on to the next one.

PART TWO - Execution

CHAPTER 4 - Get That Money Down! Cash or Financing?

Now that you have constructed your marching orders, it is time to put your money where your mouth is and seek out the financing you need to bring the project to life. The initial question you must answer is how to access the cash you need, which will ultimately come from financing or cash.

If you are fortunate enough to have saved a significant amount of cash for the project, this part of the planning may seem like a no-brainer; why pay someone else to borrow their money when you can pay for it yourself? However, even for those with a substantial amount of cash, using it to finance the house may not be the best idea. To answer this initial question, you should look at the following:

Interest Rates

One of the important things to consider in construction loans is that they customarily hold significantly higher interest rates than conventional mortgages.

The reason behind this is that the construction process brings increased risk to the bank, as when the money is provided, the project is nothing more than a hole in the ground. Thus, if the construction project fails, they are not left with the full value of the anticipated collateral to collect their debt, which ultimately means they can lose significant money.

As a result, banks are less willing to finance construction loans without significant guarantees, and their mortgage rates are upwards of twice the rate of a standard mortgage. As of May 9, 2020, the average construction loan rate was 9.75%.

The standard strategy on construction financing is to finance the construction for the short term, normally 2 years or less. When you have a finished product, pay off the construction loan with a conventional 15- or 30-year mortgage. This allows you flexibility and the ability to lower your interest rate when rates being offered are good.

Ultimately, this means that you will pay more in the short term, but if interest rates for standard mortgages remain at their current historic lows (3.15% for 15 years and 3.51% for 30 years as of May 9, 2020), you will have reasonable monthly payments. You can use that stashed cash for other purposes such as infrastructure upgrades or to serve as a rainy-day fund.

Down Payment

If you choose to go through the financing route, you will still be under an obligation to come up with a substantial down payment on the loan. Most banks require between 10 and 20% of the total loan to be paid by the debtor in cash.

The main reason for this is to reassure the bank that you have taken the process seriously enough, and you can save a substantial amount of money to put towards the project. The less down payment you can provide, the less likely a bank is willing to take a chance on you to finance the project.

Bank Locally? Or With a Chain?

This book is not meant to question an individual's financial decisions on who they bank with. However, for the sake of efficiency and the sake of your local community, you should apply for financing locally.

Most local banks and credit unions make their loan decisions in house. This means that you will receive a quicker response than if you sought financing at a national chain.

Despite the press headlines some national banks have made in recent years, there is also a practical side to using a local bank. Decisions for financing for national chains normally start locally, but the actual decision making for the financing is made either at a regional headquarters or even the national office.

This means that your application, along with the supporting documents, will be reviewed locally, and then sent to another office where it will be pooled with the other applications in that region. The banker who makes the decision does not know you any more than any of the other applicants. You are merely a series of numbers.

Meanwhile, if you have developed a relationship with a local bank, they don't only know you from the numbers you provide, but also as a person. They know about the company you work for, the side hustles you perform, and the organizations you are involved in. In small towns, it is likely that your kids may have gone to the same schools or that they played on the same little league team.

This local knowledge allows for character-based lending to be more of a factor in their overall decision. The local banker will be able to look at you as a person and will be able to better analyze whether you are someone who is trustworthy. Even if the numbers don't quite add up, whether you are worth taking the risk on, based on your personal and professional history, a local bank can be more flexible than a big bank will be.

Preparing for Initial Bank Meeting

Before making any decision on cash or financing, an initial meeting with your prospective banker will allow you to shed some light on the decision-making process. To maximize this initial meeting, you should go in armed with the following:

1. Bids from all construction contractors from foundation to finish

2. Bids from energy producers

3. Two years of income tax returns

4. A personal finance sheet showing your current assets and liabilities

5. Appraisals of any other properties you own, showing the market value

6. Copies of your most recent mortgage statements for other properties owned.

The purpose of this meeting is to start gathering specifics of what type of financing may be available to you and what undertaking it will require to secure this financing. It is never a good idea to commit to a proposal in the first meeting, and customarily, the banker you will be meeting will need to go back to his boss before they issue any type of commitment to you to finance your project.

Efficiency in this process is important. If at all possible, the first bank meeting you have should be with the bank where you usually bank. This will provide a more direct route to approval because the bank will already have a substantial amount of information about you in their files. They will easily be able to analyze your ability to stay current on financial obligations without having to send inquiries to other financial institutions.

The Pre-Commitment Process

After you have provided sufficient information along with your application, the bank will likely make an initial determination on your credit worthiness by offering you a "Pre-Commitment" letter. This letter essentially means that the bank is interested in financing your project but has not fully committed to the idea yet. It's essentially a 'maybe' letter.

It is important not to treat this pre-commitment as an actual commitment, as there is still a reasonable possibility that after the bank runs all the numbers, they may still back out of the financing. It is only through the formal commitment process, where you sign on the dotted line, that you can be certain that you have secured the financing to begin the project. Don't make any offers on a property or start any work until you've got those papers, signed and in order.

One of the major errors overly enthusiastic off-grid purveyors may make, is to tell their contractors too early in the process that they have secured the financing for their project.

Many contractors will require a deposit before beginning work; however, some will simply move forward based on the homeowner's word. As you might imagine, this could be a big problem if you do not, in fact, secure the financing and now owe a contractor for work they've begun, but you have no way to pay for.

This process can be a recipe for disaster if, after further vetting, the bank comes back and states that they cannot proceed with the financing due to additional information that came to light after the pre-commitment letter had been issued.

If your contractor has put a month's worth of work in and now it is determined that the cash is not handy to complete the project, this could lead to the ultimate failure of your project and a wide range of potential lawsuits to follow. The contractor will expect payment in full, and you cannot blame him. They have employees to pay for the hours worked, after all.

BOTTOM LINE: DO NOT ALLOW YOUR CONTRACTOR TO BREAK GROUND UNTIL THE BANK HAS ISSUED YOU THE CHECK!

What Closing Costs Mean

One of the most common misconceptions in the financing process is the cost to close the loan. If you have ever financed a home before, you may be familiar with the HUD settlement statement that outlines all the costs associated with the loan.

This, in most cases, will include real estate taxes for an entire year, attorney's fees, homeowner's or builder's insurance, as well as any other fees that may not be so obvious, such as loan generation fees and copying costs.

Ultimately, closing costs can add thousands of dollars to the loan, which will either be required to be paid out of pocket at closing or will be added to the principal, which you will be required to pay back over time.

At upwards of 10% annual interest on construction loans, baking closing costs into the loan itself can create significant increases in the overall bottom line.

To best preview the anticipated costs, most banks are required to provide good faith estimates of what the closing costs will be before a commitment is agreed between the homeowner and bank.

As was illustrated with the initial estimate in Chapter 2, it is important to add a 10% variable to the estimated closing costs so you can be properly prepared when it is time to sign documents at the closing table.

What is Title Insurance and Why am I Required to Pay for it?

Title insurance, in real estate financing, ensures that, if there are any issues with the actual title of the property, the title insurer can step in to defend against the claim.

These types of claims are most often based on a mistake in the title quest or failure to notify the purchaser of the interest of a third party in all or part of the property. This can happen if a lien is imposed on a property while the former owner has been sued for a debt, and the debtor has sought relief in the courts by having a lien on the property. Until this lien is paid in full and the lien is released, it will remain.

Most banks require that an attorney write a title policy for the property. The premium on this policy is based on the purchase price of the property. In order to minimize risk, title insurance companies require a title report to be issued by the attorney writing the policy.

This will inform both the potential owner of the property as well as the bank of any potential issues that will need to be resolved by the seller before the closing, such as liens mentioned above. There could also be second mortgages that were not disclosed.

In order to get a rough idea of what title insurance will cost, a useful calculator can be found at https://facc.firstam.com

Understanding what language is contained in the deed and what to look for in other records that arise as a result of a title search on the proper is further explained in Chapter 5. If you don't understand your contract, do not sign it.

That is the best advice anyone will ever give you. Never be in a hurry to want something so bad that you are willing to sign your life away without understanding the details in full. This can cause you a great deal of heartache if you are unlucky.

CHAPTER 5 - Getting Legal: Permits: Deeds, Rights of Way, and Contracts

If you are fortunate enough to have secured a commitment from a bank at terms that are reasonable enough for your budget, you are still far from closing the deal until you have looked into the fine print of the transaction.

Although this book should not serve as a ringing endorsement for attorneys, hiring an experienced real estate attorney for this transaction is vital to ensure that your investment is protected. This chapter will explain all the different aspects of the purchase and building process that will require an attorney's assistance and why trying to avoid the cost of one in this process will only likely to cost you more down the road.

The Purchase and Sale Contract

No one should agree to purchase real estate without the benefit of a contract that outlines each party's obligations and rights. Although real estate agents may offer a boilerplate contract, nothing substitutes for your attorney's ability to modify the contract to fit your individual needs.

When the contract is offered after a purchase price has been agreed to, the first step in protecting your rights is to ensure that there is an agreed-upon attorney review period. This period, usually somewhere between 5-10 days, allows for the buyer's and seller's attorneys to review the contract and make changes. Only after the period has passed will the contract be enforceable.

This means that if any of the clauses adversely affect your rights under the contract, your attorney can either remove those provisions or advise you to withdraw from the contract without any legal repercussions for doing so.

Often, it will be a process of negotiation to have amendments to the contract made as well as revisions to the way things are written. Anything is possible when both parties are amicable.

The bottom line, when a contract is offered, do not sign until your attorney has reviewed it, or, if you have signed, ensure the real estate agent adds an addendum for an attorney review period. Hopefully, by this time (as provided in your running checklist), you will have made initial contact with the attorney who will represent you in this transaction

Having this professional lined up before the contract is transmitted is crucial in ensuring the overall efficiency of completing this step of the project.

In evaluating the contract with your attorney, some of the key components of the contract should include:

- **Inspection Contingency**: This allows the buyer to inspect the property and, if there is a serious defect, allows them to withdraw from the contract within a prescribed time. This can be especially important if it is determined that the property contains chemical waste that will need to be cleaned up before the building process begins. This cost could be high and time-consuming. However, if you have the right to withdraw based on this discovery, you can move on to another property, or you can negotiate a lower purchase price to compensate you for paying for the cleanup yourself.

- **Financing Contingency**: Although you may have secured a commitment from a bank at the time you have been handed the proposed purchase and sale contract, this does not mean that the bank is required to go through with the deal if they find issues regarding the property's value or condition. Be sure to read all the fine print of the loan acceptance and also be sure that there is a way for you to back out of a contract if the bank gets cold feet.

- **Title Inspection Contingency:** In some cases, an attorney title search will review significant defects in the marketability of the title of the property. Liens, judgments, civil complaints, as well as a wide range of other potential encumbrances can all have a significant impact on you being able to secure the title at closing. It is important that your contract contains a title search provision that allows you to identify and force the seller to remedy defects that are discovered during the title search. If the seller cannot do so, this gives you the right to withdraw from the contract.

- **Permit Contingency:** A less common but equally important provision in the contract for the purchase of land is a permit contingency. If you intend to build your off-grid home on vacant land, you need to first ensure that the state and local agencies will allow you to do so. Wastewater permits for a septic system, as well as local requirements, which may hinder or outright eliminate the possibility that you can build the home in the area which you desire. It is important to understand these permitting issues before you follow through with the deal. Therefore, a contingency that allows you to withdraw from the contract if a permit is determined not to be issued is an important safety net to have.

Seeking Permission to Build

One of the biggest variables in the real estate development process is seeking and receiving local and state approval to build on the site you propose. Each town has different regulations and requirements that must be met before building. Some of the most important parts of the process are seeking approval to build your septic, which requires a state-issued permit.

Due to the varying regulations in each state that apply to off-grid homes, you must enlist the services of a knowledgeable real estate attorney early in the process so that they may advise and assist you in dealing with applying for securing the proper permits from the proper agencies.

Although the descriptions are meant to assist you in understanding the permit process and the requirement you may need to fulfill before breaking ground, they should not be considered an exclusive list. This again reinforces the need to consult with an attorney to ensure that there are no missed steps in this vital process.

Building Permit

Regardless of whether you are starting new construction or remodeling an existing structure, a local building permit will be required before starting construction. The building permit serves as general oversight over all facets of the construction. Most permits come with stipulations that require the builder to seek other permits as a contingency on the approval of the building permit (such as wastewater).

Depending on each municipality's requirements, they may require a professional site and building plan to be produced before they rule on the permit application. This may entail an engineering study, landscape, or building architect to construct the actual plans for the construction, while others merely require a rough sketch of what the building will look like.

To ensure you are saving money, visit the town or city planning division website before filling out the application. The information in the application, as well as the regulations that go along with the process, should sufficiently educate you to determine exactly what the application process will entail with regards to site plans.

Is there ambiguity in the application and regulations that have you guessing? Simply call the planning commissioner or clerk to clarify. It may be the best call you make all week if it resolves any lingering questions that you cannot answer on your own.

The Hearing Before the Local Commission

After the application has been submitted, there is likely to be a hearing held before the board issuing a decision. This is an opportunity for abutting property owners as well as general members of the public to comment on the proposed project.

You should in no way treat this hearing as merely a formality in receiving your final ok from the board. These hearings can be fraught with peril if you are not properly prepared. Never take anything for granted and assume that neighbors will be happy about your project.

Do I come with an Attorney?

Most commission hearings do not require that you come with an attorney. However, depending on the complexity of the project and the questions that you anticipate being asked about the overall goals of the project, coming with a well-prepared attorney may be a great insurance policy to ensure permit approval.

Keep in mind that most of these commissions are either elected through local elections or are serving in a volunteer capacity. What this ultimately means is that these boards can be wildly unpredictable.

What may seem like a shoo-in can be dumped on end and leave you having to go back to the drawing board completely. In off-grid situations, some municipalities will require that you jump through hoops not to be hooked to power. Some will require you to be tied to city water with septic systems, putting the kibosh on your compost toilet plans.

Perhaps you have a member who is having a bad day or someone who simply does not like those who attempt to buck the national trend by disconnecting from the power grid. The bottom line, you simply do not know what may happen, so take nothing for granted. If the commission denies your permit, you either have to spend a lot of time and resources refining your plan or appeal their decision to the courts. Neither of these potential outcomes is desirable, cheap, or guaranteed.

Thus, it is important that when you go into this hearing, you are ready to put forth a clear record of the grounds for your application to be approved. You should make a good impression, be respectful, and show that you are prepared.

Wastewater Permit

If your off-grid home will be serviced by a public septic system, this part of the approval permitting process may not be required. However, for those looking to install their septic, you cannot start the septic construction until you have secured the wastewater permit.

What is a Wastewater Permit?

Simply put, a wastewater permit allows you to install a system that deals with all your human waste, gray water, and run-off. These permits will often require a site inspection by an approved septic inspector who will be able to test the ground to ensure that there is a suitable location to install the septic system. This is called a perk test.

For instance, if your land is full of rock and the only area that is not is near a protected marsh area, you may not be able to build septic on the land in an area conducive to the environment. This alone may be grounds for permit denial. You may have other options, but they will likely be very costly compared to the septic system.

As outlined above, the unknown variable is one of the many reasons why it is important to gather information regarding the proposed land purchase before you close on the deal. This will ensure that hidden hazards such as insufficient land for septic will not arise after it is too late to withdraw from the deal. You might have the land perk tested or research to see if it has ever failed a perk test before.

Understand your Home State's Regulations Before Consulting with an Attorney

For the sake of efficiency, you do not want to go into your initial attorney consultation without any understanding of the permitting process. Remember, attorneys bill by the hour, regardless of whether they are advising you on things you can easily research on the State website or dealing with more complex issues with the permitting process.

Each state should have its agency of natural resources website or similarly named agency that has valuable information on the permitting process. If you familiarize yourself with the State's application, instead of asking how to apply, you can use your attorney to verify what you need to apply for instead of how you need to apply.

This preparation changes a 2-hour initial consultation into a 30 minute one. At upwards of $300 per hour, coming prepared can result in substantial savings in legal costs, which you can then apply to the cost of obtaining the actual permit.

There is no point in spending money on anything that is avoidable, and you can put that money to good use later once you're building your cabin and planting your first garden.

Understanding the Deed - Devil in the Details

The real estate deed controls how real estate changes hands. The language in the deed itself may be confusing to the layperson, which makes it that much more important to have an understanding of what goes into the deed before you close.

Although an experienced real estate attorney should be able to guide you in the process of the real estate deed analysis, reading the fine print in a deed is an important exercise to maximize your current and long-term efficiency.

The fine print is what you should pay the most attention to because the details are often burning in the fine print. Knowing these details is crucial to ensuring that you are protecting yourself and your investment.

Not only does the deed describe the parties involved in the transaction, but it also should provide sufficient details on the property itself to educate the buyer on exactly what they are buying.

There should be a legal description of the property with clearly determined corners of the property, as determined by GPS coordinates. Be sure that any land you purchase has already been surveyed and pinned so that you can locate these corner markers. This can save you thousands of dollars in boundary disputes with neighbors in the future.

The Warranty Deed - the Gold Standard in Property Transfers

A warranty deed in legal terms is a deed that contains promises from the seller that they have good and marketable title to the property they are selling. Further, a warranty deed provides that should there be an issue raised by a third party, the seller will defend against the claim to ensure that the buyer is protected. This saves you the court fees should this happen.

In most cases where bank financing is involved, a warranty deed is required. In most purchase and sale contracts, there is a requirement that the seller produce a warranty deed at closing. Although a warranty deed may be expected, it does not guarantee that it will be produced.

This is just another reason why you need to ensure that you and your counsel have time to review and modify a purchase and sale contract before it becomes enforceable.

The Quitclaim Deeds - Buyers Beware!

There is nothing more fraught with potential legal peril than the transfer of a quitclaim deed at closing.

When a seller produces a quitclaim deed, they are guaranteeing nothing. They are not even promising that they can convey the land that is described in the deed. All the buyer is saying is that whatever they own in this general vicinity, they are granting it to the seller.

In other words, it may not even be the specific plot of land that you went to see. It could be a mile away or the lot next door or a land-locked parcel that has no guaranteed access to the land for you to even get to your land.

It likely hasn't been surveyed, and that is costly to have done, and if a neighbor has already put up fences across the land that you have bought, you'll have a legal battle on your hands to get those fences removed.

Although a quitclaim deed has legitimate value in certain cases, like when a property is changing hands for no consideration, the quitclaim has no place in purchasing real estate for your off-grid home. Stay away from it.

The bottom line, if all the seller can offer is a quitclaim deed to the property you wish to purchase, do not do it unless you are 100% certain of what it is you are receiving.

There are scams happening where people are selling land with a quitclaim deed and then disappearing quickly. People are moving to the land only to be hit with an eviction notice from the actual property owner who has no idea who they are or why they are on his/her property.

Administrator or Executor's Deed

Another common deed is the deed that transfers real estate through an estate. These deeds are commonly signed by an executor named in a will who has been tasked by the language of the will to liquidate the real estate.

Although the individual owner has passed, a buyer can still be assured by the executor as an extension of the estate that they can transfer the real estate as described. As is the case with other transactions, ensure that the deed WARRANTS AND DEFENDS title. You also want to ensure that the probate court, which presides over the estate, has granted permission before the transfer. If the court has not granted this license, you are facing a significant risk of a beneficiary of the estate coming back and contesting the transfer.

Rights-of-Way Define Who Else Can Access the Property

It is common in the deed description for there to be references to a third party's right to access the property that is being conveyed.

Commonly this has to do with power utility rights to access pre-existing infrastructure that has either already been installed on the property or for which a road has been built so they can access the infrastructure on another parcel of land. Rights of way can also grant access to the parcel by individuals or businesses who may have interests in neighboring parcels.

The major issue in evaluating rights of way is to analyze where exactly the right of way is so you can ensure that you are not building your off-grid home in that area.

Some of these rights of way are decades old and are not visible on the property. However, this does not invalidate the right; it only muddies the waters, making it increasingly important to understand this restriction on your deed before purchasing.

PART THREE: Building

CHAPTER 6: Construction - What Can You Do to Maximize Efficiency?

Chances are, if you are planning to live off-grid, you are looking to lessen your carbon footprint by utilizing as much human power as you can welcome into your project. Off-grid and hand-built homes are growing as trends, even in less rural areas.

Since this is such a growing trend, strong, able-bodied folks who are interested in the experience of building an off-grid home may be willing to volunteer to join the experience and share skills. With this being said, putting up flyers, advertising on Facebook Marketplace, Craigslist, and similar forums could generate a glorious bounty of interesting individuals who may, along with free or bartered labor, bring a variety of skills and knowledge to your project.

Depending on your area, the types of knowledge about sustainable building methods will vary. However, compared to a decade ago, off-grid building and design are more common, and many general contractors now have the experience, including off-grid concepts into their designs.

If you are interested in learning on your own, there are a handful of schools that offer graduate programs in ecological design, as well as some smaller training programs that offer short classes in sustainable building practices and tiny home construction.

Beyond the wholesome nature that may be provided for those seeking off-grid living, there is also the practicality surrounding self-sufficiency and what that means for your bottom line.

As our back of the napkin math has shown, which is likely further emphasized by your performance of the running task list, off-grid homes can be as or more expensive than a traditional home.

Although the costs may be technically comparable, this chapter is meant to stimulate ideas on how you can save on certain expenses such as building materials and labor. The most cost-efficient way for you to build your off-grid home is for you to be able to assist in the building process in any way possible.

Not only will this save you money on professional labor, it will also allow you to become more intimately knowledgeable about the details of the home as it is being built.

Find a Builder Who Will Also Act as a Teacher

One of the first questions you should ask your building contractor is whether they will allow you to tag along as they go through the building process. By observing how certain aspects of your home are built, you are building your knowledge base on what it will take to repair these parts of the home when the aging process begins to deteriorate certain parts of the home.

When the time comes to repair certain parts of your off-grid home, you will have the knowledge to do it yourself, which saves you the call to the contractor to perform the labor for you. Not only does this save you a substantial amount of money, it also enriches your off-grid living experience.

Knowledge is certainly power, and in this case, this knowledge equates to big-time savings, so do not be afraid to inquire from your builder if he is willing to teach you while you are also offering him an extra hand to help.

Beyond learning the building process, you can also be a real asset to the efficiency of building your home by taking care of the mundane tasks that consume a large part of the builder's days.

Runs to the dump to dispose of materials, landscaping, and clean-up duties are all important tasks that you can easily perform to assist in the flow of the project. Performing these tasks will save you money in avoiding having to pay a third party while also freeing up time to allow the builders to focus more of their energy on the complex tasks of building the home.

It may be a good idea to have an initial consultation with the builder on exactly what role you will play in assisting them in the building process. Come to a clear understanding of what you should and should not be doing throughout the process.

Although helping with the basic tasks of the building process can be quite helpful, what may be counterproductive is if you step on other's toes while you're doing it.

The old adage of *'too many cooks in the kitchen'* certainly applies to home building as well, so make sure the directions are clear prior to you taking on too many tasks that may, in fact, restrict the building process instead of freeing it up.

Some builders are not keen to have the homeowner involved in the process for this very reason, and this is why you should work it out beforehand. It can also cramp their style when the homeowner gets overly involved and attempts to change the design at the last minute.

For the contractor, having someone ask to change the layout of the bathroom at the last minute is a major pain, and it won't go far in building a great relationship with your construction manager if you are constantly attempting to do this.

If he asks you for input, that's one thing, but otherwise, don't try to make last-minute changes and improvements to your plan.

Timber

Depending on the amount of time you have and the available space, you might want to consider harvesting your lumber from your land. It is becoming increasingly accessible for landowners to get a hold of a simple sawmill or rent or hire a portable mill to use on their land. This requires a significant amount of planning because the wood will need to cure prior to it being cut.

There are several ways to "cure" lumber, which is just a technical word for "drying," and each may take some time. Location is something to consider here because depending on the average level of humidity in your area and average yearly rainfall, this process can take upwards of six months for your green lumber to dry naturally.

Without an existing structure on your land, the lumber will need to sit outside for the entirety of the drying period unless it is kiln-dried. Kiln drying cuts the process down significantly from several weeks to about a month.

A solar kiln is something you can build right on your property to house the wood and allow for it to dry using solar power, decreasing drying time. All of this reduces your carbon footprint and avoids supporting lumber companies that may use harmful harvesting practices.

Straw Bale Homes

A friend of mine grew up in a straw bale home. I used to make jokes with her about whether the big bad wolf could huff and puff and blow her house down. She assured me that it was probably sturdier than my house!

As I grew up and became more interested in ecological building styles, I learned more about how straw bale houses are built. The house is built by framing the entire house structure and forming the walls by stacking and securing straw bales with ropes and wood framing materials.

The walls provide some support, but mainly serve as an insulation. Then the bales are covered in plaster, allowing for the walls to be waterproof but breathable. This process requires significantly less effort than building a cob or straw/clay home and provides a similar, if not better, level of insulation that can keep a house at an ambient temperature year-round with great efficiency.

The most challenging aspect of this building style is securing a good source of straw, having it delivered to the property depending on location, and keeping it perfectly dry during the building process.

This challenge extends to keeping the house under cover while the plaster coating dries. The last thing you want in a house like this is mold. You are completely beholden to mother nature with this style of architecture. While not impossible to accomplish in a humid environment, you will have a much easier time in a warm, dry climate.

One perk of straw bale homes is that you can do a lot of the work yourself, saving thousands on construction labor. There are many online resources and available classes and schools in different parts of the country that can teach you the skills needed to build a straw bale home.

Cob/Wattle and Daub

An ancient building method, *Cob*, originated in England in Wales. Some of them still exist, as cob structures have been standing for several centuries. Cob is a mixture of clay, sand, rock, and straw.

The builder mixes the earthen materials with water and straw on a big tarp(usually mixing with their feet) and either form bricks with this material, fill previously built frames, "wattle and daub" (a historic European building method using woven sticks to create a framed wall which is filled with *clay, sand, earth, straw* and sometimes...*animal dung*), or just hand build your home by layering slabs of this material and sculpting as you go.

Cob houses are often described charmingly as "hobbit huts" regarding their aesthetics because they have smoothed corners and sometimes flowing extremities as a stylish attribute.

There has been a significant resurgence with the trend of sustainable building practices, with more modern design concepts and ideas available to help you decide whether this style is the one for you.

The beauty of this building style is that it's relatively simple, so pretty much anyone can learn how to build a cob home in a very short time, and the materials can be locally sourced or purchased for very little.

Similar challenges exist when building with Cob or Straw Clay, as you may experience with the straw bale home. The builder is constantly fighting against humidity until the home is completely dry. Cob, however, allows the builder to build heat pipes throughout the structure of the home, which in turn helps the home to dry much faster from the inside out.

Cob homes are some of the most efficient homes concerning heating and cooling. Oftentimes, a Cob home can be heated year-round with very little wood and using a small rocket stove (more on Rocket Stoves later) along with some strategically placed wood stove piping. The builder can install a couch or bed platform around the exit pipes from the stove, so they can sit or sleep on the warm surface.

Oregon Cob is a more contemporary style of cob building that was developed in Oregon to accommodate for wetter climates (such as the Pacific Northwest). This method was designed to use less material by building thinner walls with a more precise mixture of clay and sand, along with more straw to create a stronger structure using less.

These thinner walls dry quicker, cost less, and are potentially stronger than traditional cob styles. With these thinner walls, however, you compromise the amount of heat that can be held within the structure of the building, and therefore these homes may be less cost-efficient to heat.

Some of the disadvantages of Cob homes are they are pretty much the finished product. It is challenging to do any renovations on them without destroying them completely.

Cob houses can be repaired, however, using the same materials built on top of itself, so minor repairs and adjustments are quite easy. Also, very careful planning and design are required for this method with regards to wiring and plumbing before building because you build the walls around these networks as you go.

Thermal mass is a term used when talking about cob structures, but this does not necessarily mean insulation. Cob can hold heat and distribute it efficiently around a home that is well designed for this purpose. However, it is not the best insulator.

A combination of straw bale walls and a cob interior can utilize the efficiency of the thermal mass that cob provides while improving the efficiency of the straw bale interior.

Stone

Stone requires a lot of man or machine power to incorporate into your structure. One way to build an efficient stone home is to frame the complete structure, leaving gaps in the frame, which will function as molds for the stone and concrete. While this is a quicker way to build with stone, it may not be the most aesthetically pleasing.

Essentially, you dump a large number of rocks into the framed "walls" and then pour concrete down atop them, allowing it to settle into the crevices. This can produce a beautiful effect in some areas, but not others due to the unruly nature of the spreading of the concrete.

Historically, stone homes were built by hand, and the stones were picked carefully and placed in such a way that the formation of the rock wall would provide support, and concrete was just the glue to bring the rocks into place.

The benefit of a stone house, other than they are beautiful and "otherworldly," is that the insulation potential is immense. Although it may be a challenge to heat up depending on the size of the home, stone holds heat extremely well as well as cold.

Recycled materials

Many recycled or upcycled materials can be used to save time and money. Most areas have local building materials/housewares salvage companies that sell bits and pieces for a fraction of the cost you would face in buying new ones.

Materials such as doors, windows, cabinets, sinks, you name it, have been salvaged from houses that have gutted or torn down. It's always good to look into these places well before you start building. The availability of materials may influence many decisions along the way.

Shipping Containers

You may have read about a new trend of tiny houses made out of shipping containers. Although these houses are aesthetically industrial, they are extremely affordable. This is because they are fully contained when they arrive. They require no manpower to create the structure, and you can work year-round at renovating the inside right from the time it arrives on your land.

Shipping container homes are so popular; they can even be purchased, fully designed, and ready to move into on Amazon. The buying options for tiny homes and specifically shipping container homes have been booming in the last few years.

These homes come in 2 sizes: 20 by 8 or 40 by 8, similar to a common trailer. Interestingly enough, these also are stackable, and you can hop down the Google rabbit hole for a variety of attractive stacked designs.

Purchasing a shipping container home designed and ready to go can be quite efficient and affordable, so you don't have to worry about the design process and all of the trial and error that comes along with it. It all depends on how involved you want to be in the creative process, which, however, can actually be the most exciting part.

Many municipalities have special building codes for shipping container homes because once the metal is cut, they lose a lot of their structural integrity. It's essential that proper methods of framing are used to ensure that the buildings don't collapse as the work is being done or after construction is complete.

Tiny homes, Homes on Wheels, and Conversions

Any version of the home you are dreaming of can be built in a tiny version or a rolling version. From an old airstream to a school bus, a tiny home can give you the freedom of your own space while seriously cutting expenses. Tiny homes are structurally compact and can provide an aesthetic beauty of a much larger home for a significantly lower price.

A majority of the time can be either recycled completely or made from recycled or found materials. In the U.S, the size considered to be a tiny home is between 100 and 400 square feet or $\frac{1}{6}$ of the size of a conventional home.

Now living in a space this small definitely requires significant planning and downsizing of possessions. Some people choose to use a storage unit for belongings until they have had adequate time in their tiny home to determine if it is safe to sell their furniture and excess possessions.

There are many unique ways to incorporate storage into a well-designed tiny home, but regardless of the clever locations of the storage compartments, you will seriously have to consider which possessions are worth weeding out depending on the size and type of tiny home you choose. It's a big decision and trying the tiny home on for size first might be a good idea.

Tiny homes are perfect for many people, while others find them too small and restrictive. They certainly are a great way to reduce your footprint and also be free to travel if your tiny house on wheels (THOW) is towable to the next destination.

Be it stationary or a rolling home, the tiny home is gaining in popularity because it can allow the builder the freedom of having a home of their own but on a limited budget. If the tiny home is a rolling home, it can allow freedom to change location without having to move any of your stuff. Younger Americans are in love with tiny homes.

They can live near college campuses and easily relocate after graduation. Moving to an expensive metro area is not as out of reach if their home is portable and paid-off. A self-built tiny home can be built for cash, one piece at a time. Even using recycled items and upcycled goods can put this type of home well into anyone's budget.

Types of Homes on Wheels

Campers

The standard rolling home is an actual camper or camper van. These are designed for vacation living, set up to hook up to water, sewer, and electric systems and already have everything you need to live. Newer ones obviously have more modern technology with regards to the amenities you might want in a rolling home, but even older campers can be upgraded fairly easily.

Older campers such as the popular airstream can be found in a spectrum of different conditions depending on how much you would like to spend. These can also be easily gutted and remodeled inside with your own design. Most of these camper styles are not winterized, so modifications to increase insulation would be necessary if you were planning to overwinter in one of these.

Trailers

There is a growing trend now of tiny rolling homes built atop flatbed trailers. This concept allows for endless design possibilities regarding size, style, and efficiency. There are a variety of different flatbed trailers to choose from, starting with a conventional flatbed trailer to fiberglass trailers, specifically designed to improve fuel economy.

The materials you choose to build your rolling home can certainly affect fuel economy as well. For instance, fir is a light wood that has the highest strength to weight ratio of all the North American softwoods.

Additionally, for the roof, fiberglass, as used on boats, can be used here as a weather-resistant but light material to take the place of a conventional roof. Depending on the size and intentional use of your rolling home, the possibilities are endless when you start with a blank flatbed as a canvas.

Conversions

Finally, there are many different other conversions that can be made to conventional vehicles such as buses, vans, and even pick-up truck beds. A wide variety of designs can be built inside or on just about any type of vehicle you have the vision to convert.

The challenges with converting existing vehicles into rolling homes are that you must rely on the state of the mechanical components of the vehicle to ensure the longevity of the mobility of your home. Oftentimes, affordable vehicles that are structurally sound enough to gut and convert inside and out into a rolling home are older, used vehicles (they just don't make vehicles like they used to).

More modern vehicles are made out of a significant amount more plastic than older vehicles, and that is not the best material to build a rolling home into or on (because of the age). However, these vehicles may have a lot of wear and tear on the engines and other mechanical components.

This does not mean there are not well-kept school buses for sale that can easily be converted into rolling homes, but it may take some shopping around and some trips to the mechanic to build your dream conversion vehicle.

Some Additional Things to Consider:

Many decisions make up the off-grid construction project. Regardless of aesthetics, there will be many questions to ask yourself regarding the practicality of your endeavor based on your location, budget, available materials and time, and whether or not you plan to design and build your home yourself or hire an experienced contractor.

Some basic components of your off-grid home remain constant across all styles of structures. Components of your project such as Water, Sewer, Power, and Heat, and your needs based on geographic location and climate may aid in your design decision making before you even decide on any of the aesthetics.

All the structures listed in this chapter can be equipped with all of the amenities necessary for a home, depending on your level of need and your location.

CHAPTER 7: The Pros and Cons of a Tiny House

In today's society, humans live very complicated lives: long work weeks, numerous debts, and monthly expenses, as well as the accumulation of material possessions. We have large sections of our homes as well as extra buildings dedicated to just storage.

The things that we store are not things that we are using daily, but the things we keep for later, things we hold onto for sentimental value, the clothing we might fit into again, or some useful things that we might need someday.

Media popularity of minimizing possessions and decluttering our homes through television shows, books, and blogs, has recently shown that our continuous accumulation of possessions, that essentially only lead to clutter in our lives, is stressing us out.

We dream of simpler lives where we don't have to work as much for all of these possessions and to keep up our properties as we fight against mother nature to repair, replace and rebuild aging structures.

It's a losing battle and quite often ends up being unmanageable and fails, to the expense of our mental and physical health with very little time for leisure.

When we think of living inside a tiny home, quite often being used too much larger amounts of household space, we may find it impossible to imagine being able to function. However, as we learn to minimize and keep only the things that we need and use every day, a form of order comes to our lives; one that can relieve us of the great burden of responsibility we carry to repeatedly re-organize large mounds of possessions, and further cultivate the psychological need to buy more.

It doesn't happen overnight to wrap your brain around such an endeavor, but by letting go of material possessions that just hold space in our homes and our psyches, and by making the decision to only keep what is useful, not only clears our living space but also clears our minds. New science has come out in the past decade that shows that clutter causes anxiety.

Cluttered homes cause a continued spike in the stress hormone cortisol (which has been linked to obesity and numerous health problems) and causes it to continue to spike throughout the day. Workers are much more productive in spaces free from clutter. If cluttered immediate surroundings cause us great stress, think of an entire home filled with useless stuff accumulating by the year that surrounds us as it grows and grows, as we work longer hours to buy more of it.

Then we imagine a life free from these huge expenses when we can have time to spend on creative projects, time to spend with family and friends. Also, the time we don't have to spend repairing, organizing, and moving around our possessions that we forgot we had, and quite potentially are still paying for having charged them on our credit cards.

In a tiny home, these trials may still exist to an extent, but along with the decision to live in a tiny home comes a philosophical change. Experiencing the simplistic beauty of a minimalist lifestyle can add years to your life by freeing up living space and brain space for the peace and tranquility of freedom from complexities that we are so used to enduring, that they have become normal.

Tiny homes became a growing trend in the 60s when the back to the land movement began in the northeast and the Pacific northwest. People began dreaming of living on communal land with low overhead and living expenses. Even tree houses became popular as living spaces and have shown new popularity in recent times.

Lloyd Kahn, a modern tiny-home and fitness guru has published many books on tiny homes and living spaces, highlighting a variety of tiny homes spanning decades and across the world. With so many resources in these building styles, there are endless design concepts for tiny house dwelling so that you can customize your small space to fit your lifestyle and location.

Financing

One big way to save money by living in a tiny home is general financing. Most tiny home dwellers do not hold mortgages on their houses, and therefore save thousands of dollars on the interest that they would have paid for mortgages for much larger homes.

Unless you are purchasing land, the loans to construct tiny homes are too low to meet the minimum for a conventional mortgage. This situation is not ideal because personal loans carry high-interest rates in comparison to mortgages, so in the end, if you don't have the cash up front to build a tiny home, you will be paying a ton in just interest.

Adapting to Smaller Spaces

Design is most important when making the decision to transition to live in a tiny home. Think of where you would like to spend the most time and make sure you do not compromise that space in your design. While small, the tiny house can be very comfortable if designed properly. Care must be taken to ensure you can move through your space with ease and will feel comfortable. This being said, if you are used to having guests over regularly, indoor seating will be extremely limited, no matter your design. It can take some time getting used to it when suddenly you just have less available space.

You will be doing laundry more often, washing dishes more often, and needing to return things to their place to maintain a sense of order in such a small space. But these tasks will take a fraction of the time they once did before downsizing. As we will mention later, you will also notice that living expenses with regards to heating, cooling, and general upkeep will be next to nothing compared to living in an average to larger sized home.

Storage

Storage can be a puzzle when designing a tiny home, but a creative one at that. You will need to get rid of or store separately a good majority of your belongings before jumping into a tiny house living situation.

However, there are many storage compartment ideas online about how to design the interior of your tiny home with a dual purpose in mind, such as using staircases (which can incorporate pocket shelves underneath the staircase, as well as drawers beneath each stair) for storage.

Incorporating plenty of wall shelving helps with space. If you want to keep a lot of stuff, you are going to have to get creative with storage. Additionally, if your tiny home is of the rolling variety, you will be seriously concerned with weight most of all. Therefore, your personal possessions will need to be carefully chosen.

Taxes and Living Expenses. Are Tiny Homes Cheaper?

The Expense of Building a Tiny Home

Depending on the materials you choose for building, a tiny house can cost as little as $10,000 to $12,000 to build. Compared to the average price to build a conventional home, which is as costly as $200,000.

Because the square footage of the tiny home is so small, the tiny home can often be built with mostly reclaimed, recycled, or natural materials that can be purchased for a fraction of the cost of buying new materials.

The biggest expenses, other than contractor fees, and depending on the style, lie in the utilities: sewer, plumbing, electrical, and heating systems, including solar panels. Once the house is built, there are various regular expenses such as taxes, heating, cooling, and maintenance.

Most tiny home dwellers spend as little as $10 to $35 a month for all utilities. This makes these homes attainable for any budget. Solar homes, depending on the location, will cost nothing for electricity and sometimes hot water. However, if you live in a place where it isn't sunny all year long, you will have an added cost of fueling a generator during the dark months.

Property Taxes

Property taxes are one of the reasons one might gravitate toward owning a tiny home. If your tiny home is on wheels, you will not have to worry about paying property taxes at all unless it is parked on the property that you own.

If yours is a rolling home, you get the freedom to move away whenever you wish. Typically, rolling home dwellers would enter into a lease agreement with the landowner, essentially renting a parking spot wherever they decide will be their temporary home.

Additionally, mobile or rolling homes can be parked at state parks and other spots set up for mobile living, and then you just pay the fees while you are there.

This is also a great time to remind you that a home on wheels is not considered a permanent improvement on the land, and therefore, will not increase your property taxes if you own the land. Park your tiny home where it is allowed and enjoy the life of the country without the increase in taxes.

Water, Sewer, and Electricity

There are a variety of creative ways to tackle basic amenities in a tiny home. A lot of tiny homes use minimal resources for heating, cooling, and energy.

Solar power is perfect for the tiny home as it will need only a few solar panels to achieve the energy needed for both electricity and hot water. A stationary tiny home will either connect to a municipal system for water and sewer or, similar to a conventional home, will have a dug well or sewer.

Rolling homes, however, will require a storage container for both water and sewer, in addition to having hookups to tap into water sources on the road. One way to bypass the septic storage would be to install a composting toilet.

These come in various sizes and styles. As we will address later in Act 3, they can either be anywhere from very primitive to very sophisticated and almost like a conventional toilet. Either way, your burden on a system for these purposes will be extremely light in a tiny home.

Heating and cooling

It is extremely efficient to heat a tiny home. Since the space is much smaller, you have the less square footage to heat, and with certain insulation and heating techniques, you can keep warm on next to nothing with regards to resources.

The best way to heat a tiny home is with a wood stove or pellet stove. They come in a wide range of sizes and styles, and more modern stoves burn very efficiently, so you can set them to recirculate the smoke within to harness the heat from the coals of the wood following the burn.

In addition, as discussed in the section on cob architecture, this material can be used in thermal mass and requires only a small rocket stove (a small, 2-part stove listed later, which uses small diameter wood for fuel to produce high heat output at a low cost) to heat a small space efficiently. Some tiny homes use conventional heaters such as propane or gas.

Groceries

We already mentioned the lack of storage, so a change in lifestyle is advised when thinking of tiny house living. Included in the topic of storage is food storage. Depending on how many people are living in your tiny home, you probably won't be able to store as much food inside your home as you would in a conventional home.

This implies more regular visits to the grocery store and services. If you're like me and you shop regularly during the week, that's not going to be a concern. If you pick a remote place to locate your tiny house, you'll do a longer trek more often. This will, however, stress your piggy bank with regard to gas, unless you can ride or walk, which also restricts your ability to shop for more than a few days.

Laundry

The likelihood of your desire to compromise your already limited space in your tiny home with a washer and dryer is slim. Therefore, another trip you will be making will be to the laundromat. This could potentially cost more in laundromat fees and fuel for travel.

There are some portable clothes washer options out there for folks looking to live in a more primitive style, but if you are not into hand washing and line drying, you're going to have to go to the laundromat. Also, because you will have significantly downsized your wardrobe due to the lack of available closet space, your trips to do laundry will be more frequent.

Appliances

It would be a waste of already limited space to install a full-sized refrigerator and stove into your tiny kitchen, so there will be some shopping to do with regard to choosing the appliances to install.

With so many to choose from, you will need to decide which attributes of tiny home appliances you would like to focus on with regard to energy use, size, and price.

These smaller appliances, since they are not standard models, are not much cheaper than their full-sized versions but can save you a lot of money in the long run by their efficiency standards.

For instance, a solar refrigerator/freezer in the mini variety could cost you around $1,100 brand new, but the energy savings will allow for the appliance to pay for itself in the long run. Stove ranges are more reasonable for the size, and you can get a 20" range in either propane or electric between $500 and $600. However, if you are looking to go solar in your tiny home, propane would be the way to go, especially during the darker months, so setting up your home with a propane hook up would be necessary.

As far as laundry goes, it is unlikely that you would want to designate any of your already limited space to a washer and dryer. However, there are some efficient and user-friendly portable clothes washers to fill in the gaps between trips to the laundromat.

If you cannot let go of in-home laundry, you can choose between some fairly pricey options for RV washer and dryer combos, which are either stackable or all in one to save space.

There are a lot of ways a tiny home can be a way to save money. However, the initial startup costs and purchase of appliances may be similar to that of a conventional home. You will save money on energy costs living in a tiny home no matter your climate because smaller spaces take less energy to heat and cool.

If your home is on wheels, you will save significantly on property taxes and also have the option to travel to warmer climates as the seasons change in order to avoid having to use expensive energy to heat the home.

Generally, over time, the tiny home would pay for itself in savings. Since you have only the space for necessary items, you will get out of the habit of over purchasing personal items that will eventually end up in storage.

PART FOUR - Completion

CHAPTER 8 - Water Supply

No home is complete without a safe and reliable water supply. For those who are looking to build an off-grid home in an area serviced by municipal water supply, this chapter may not apply.

However, for most off-grid homeowners, their desire to be free from public utility reliance also consists of being free from water treatment often conducted by the town public work's department.

What this means is that as part of the construction process, you need to locate the best possible water source on your property and to gauge how you wish to utilize it for your needs.

Step One - Determine Your Water Requirements

The average American uses 80-100 gallons of water per day. This statistic means that a family of four can consume over 12,000 gallons of water per month. The first step in ensuring you have a water supply sufficient to your needs is first to see if there are ways in which you can minimize the water you pull from your water source so you can alleviate the stress placed on the system. Below are a couple of easy habit-building ways to cut down on your water supply usage.

Rainfall

There are many people who question whether rainfall is suitable for consumer use in activities such as showering. Catching and using rain has long been a way for people to flush their toilets or wash their clothes; however, some have resisted the temptation to use it when it comes to personal hygiene.

Filtered rainwater is perfectly safe, and many find out that it is better than well water. Rainwater is soft water, making it a wonderful choice for showers and washing the hair. Your skin is always soft after a shower with rainwater.

Given that the average showerhead produces 2 gallons of water per minute, for a family of four, it is easy to see why recycling water for showers may be one of the most efficient ways to cut down on your water supply usage.

There are numerous resources out there that can teach you how to properly treat your rainwater collection to ensure it is safe to shower in. The major components of this process are:

- Use a sanitized storage container that is not clear to keep water safe and fresh. Clear containers encourage algae growth in the sunshine.

- Filter the water that is pumped through your plumbing to prevent mineral deposits.

- If needed, use additives to sanitize the water further. The measurements of bleach to sanitize water safely can be found https://www.thoughtco.com.

Low-Flow Appliances

Another great way to reduce your water usage is to install low flow appliances in your household. These are especially effective for showerheads as well as toilets. If installed, they can cut your water usage by up to half.

Change You Usage Habits

Although the development of technology has made the conservation of water more straightforward, there still is no substitute for modifying your behavior to cut down on water usage. Although many of these habits are self-explanatory, if you genuinely want to cut down on water usage, these simple techniques deserve constant reminding:

- Limit showers to no more than 10 minutes: We all get dirty, sweaty, and downright filthy. However, it should never take longer than 10 minutes for you to shower away the dirt. Remember that each minute in the shower expends 2 gallons of water, which means that if you turn a 20-minute shower into 10, you are saving 20 gallons of water per shower.

- Maximize Productivity While in Shower: There is no reason why you cannot take care of other bathroom tasks with the same water that you are using to shower. Bring in your toothbrush and razor. A little suction cup mirror will allow you to use the same water for brushing your teeth and shaving as you are for cleaning your body, instead of restraining the process once you leave the shower.

- Shut Water off While Brushing Teeth - There is no more significant waste of water than running the water while you brush your teeth, although many people still seem to ignore this. It's simple, it's straightforward, and it can save you a ton of water. Dampen toothbrush, shut the water off, brush teeth, turn the water on, rinse. The water should be running for no more than 20 seconds instead of the 2 minutes that of running water that is often associated with brushing your teeth.

- Place Bowl Under Sink to Catch Otherwise Wasted Water: If you place a large water bowl under the faucet, you will be able to catch a lot of the water that would otherwise go down the drain. Washing your vegetables, washing your hands, or even getting a drink of water from the faucet cause excess water to be expended. This excess water may serve a useful purpose, such as flushing a toilet or watering your plants can be caught by the bowl instead of draining into your septic system. Every bit of caught water helps and, if you are consistent with it, can add up to a lot of saved water.

- Place Bucket in Shower to Catch Water While Shower is Warming Up: Depending on your water heater, it can take upwards of one minute running for the shower water to reach a comfortable warmth. This reality means that you are wasting up to two gallons of water while you wait. Instead of watching this water go down the train, place a 5-gallon bucket in the shower to catch the water so you can use it for other tasks later.

- Recycle Water That Would Otherwise Go Down the Drain: There is a wide range of household tasks that do not require freshwater to perform. Flushing toilets, washing windows are but a few of the examples where you can use recycled water. If you have a dishpan or bathtub full of water, instead of using the water faucet, utilize this water to perform these everyday tasks. Diligence in recycling water can make a significant impact.

Choosing the Right Water Supply

Now that you have been able to determine a rough water usage outline for your home, it is time to pick the right type of independent water source that will feed your off-grid home. For homes that seek independence from public infrastructure, there are two options when it comes to choosing a water supply.

Natural Spring

A natural spring is the most efficient way to tap into a water supply that already exists on your property. If you have an abundance of fresh water on your property that feeds into your house, count your lucky stars as the harvesting of natural spring often takes a lot more analysis beyond identifying the spring's existence.

Spring needs to be carefully tapped as it can easily collapse on itself and close up. There are many states that have a plethora of natural springs available. Missouri has an extensive underground water supply that exists in underground caves and streams and sometimes bubbles up in springs. Springwater is of excellent quality as it has been naturally sand-filtered.

Test Before You Consider

Before you start to formulate even the most basic of plans for your natural spring, the first thing you need to do is test the quality of the water. Springwater can look pristine by site yet still be full of minerals, bacteria, and other contaminants that will turn your ideal spring water into an expensive hassle.

It can take as little as ten minutes to get a reading on the quality of your water, as here is an abundance of quality drinking water test kits that are on the market—testing the spring water on two occasions during two different times of the day. You do not want to risk a false reading, as this can have disastrous results if you rely on a clean test that, upon the second opinion, is determined to be incorrect.

After you have received an accurate reading on your water test, research what the ideal levels for each of the identified components of the water are. Although these tests may indicate that there is a presence of a contaminant, it may be well within the acceptable guidelines set forth by the EPA and, therefore, suitable for your water supply. Go to htttps://www.epa.gov/sites/production/files/2018-03/documents/dwtable2018.pdf for more info.

Do You Need a Water Filtration System?

If you are fortunate enough to have a pure spring water supply, the question becomes whether you should try to tamper with this water by applying a water filtration system. Ideally, the makeup of your drinking water will have the right minerals to enrich your health. If they do, you may wish to leave the water as it is.

However, if your tests reveal elevated, although acceptable levels of minerals, as well as other sediments, the use of a water filtration system may turn your adequate water into something far superior that is also safer for your plumbing.

There is a wide range of water filters available to address water quality issues. Be sure to conduct the proper research and consult with an experienced plumber or water quality expert before you commit to a water filtration system.

Where is the Spring Located?

One of the most frustrating parts of finding your water supply is finding a fresh spring that is located too close to your home in an area that is likely to interfere with your septic. Your water supply needs to be at least 100 feet from your leach field and should be located above it.

Depending on the makeup of your land, this may be difficult to achieve as it is common for there to be very few acceptable places for a leach field to be installed, which can preclude your utilization of many sources of fresh water.

Installing the Water Line

Now that you have found a spring that provides freshwater, it is time to plan the water line that will bring this water directly to your home. Ideally, the spring will be located above your home so you can let gravity do most of the work. Even if the water supply is located below your home, there are water pumps on the market that can pump the water uphill so it can feed in your home.

There are many ingenious ideas on how to utilize a pump system, some of which are more expensive than others. If you have been able to accurately gauge your family's anticipated water usage (add 10% to your estimates like in your back of the napkin math), then you can easily find a water pump that will fit your needs.

For some creative ideas on pump ideas, there are some great articles on those who have utilized low-cost systems to feed their backwoods cabins. Not only do these articles provide low-cost options, they also chart them out for you so you can understand exactly how the system works.

Regardless of whether you need a pump to assist in providing your water supply, there are a few other considerations you need to consider when running your water line from the spring to the home.

How Deep Does the Water Line Need to Be?

The major debate going on now with the burying depth of water lines is exactly how deed they need to be in order to avoid freezing. Generally speaking, it has been advised that the water line should be buried somewhere between 5-6 feet deep. This depth will get the waterline below the frost line in the ground, which will allow it to avoid freezing.

There is now a second line of thought for water lines, where instead of digging a 5-foot trench for the length of the line, you utilize a shielded water line that is buried only two feet deep. A study showed that the combination of an insulated pipe and a two-foot trench was as effective as an uninsulated pipe buried six feet deep.

The cost difference between digging a six-foot trench as opposed to a two-foot one is significant. Although it may seem like an obvious choice if the studies have shown a similar result, you should not simply begin the two-foot digging process without consulting with a professional first. What would be even more expensive than digging the six-foot trench would be if your waterline burst due to insufficient insulation, which would then require you to dig up the water line to repair the damaged pipe.

Be 100% sure that your waterline will be safe from the elements before you commit to a plan. Only through this cautious approach can you efficiently proceed to provide your house with the fresh spring water it needs.

Well

If you cannot find an adequate freshwater supply on your property, your only other option is to dig for one. Finding a well can be time-consuming and expensive, especially for land that is more arid. The variations in cost are significantly different in each state. The average cost to hire a company to dig a well can range from $3,000-$15,000.

A more accurate way to determine the cost is to measure by per-foot that is dug. Given the wide range in geological compositions of the soil across the country, it is best to use your estimates based on the state in which your off-grid home will be located. A great tool to get a per-foot estimate for digging a well in each state can be found at https://homeguide.com/costs/well-drilling-cost#location.

It is important to note that the same water testing criteria should apply with a well as with a natural spring. If you are required to dig deep to access a water supply, the need for testing becomes even more important.

Do not rush this part of the process. If it is found after digging that one area is heavy with minerals and other contaminants, you may need to find another location. Although this will increase the cost, there is no substitute for having the healthiest, cleanest water possible to serve your off-grid home.

CHAPTER 9: The Bathroom - Where and What You Need

Now that you have secured a sufficient water source that is hooked up to your home, it is time to figure out how your bathrooms will best be able to utilize the water source while also minimizing water usage. Water is a precious resource, and we must not use it without regard.

The first step in analyzing potential bathrooms is to figure out exactly how minimal you want this part of your off-grid home to play in the floor space or, if you're even more hardcore, if you want it to play any role inside the home at all. Some off-grid homes utilize outhouses and composting toilets that may be indoors or outdoors. In this section, we'll explore the many choices that you can consider.

A Discussion About Outhouses

Going to the bathroom and showering outside your home may not be an attractive idea to most persons, especially during the winter months. However, even today, outhouses can play a significant role in your bathroom designs while also cutting down on your water usage and required indoor space.

There are several styles of outhouses from which you can choose - from the moveable outhouse over a man-made hole variety, to a composting set up where you remove the waste and add it to your composting system (more on that later).

If you are considering a conventional outhouse (hole in the ground type) to accessorize your off-grid home, keep in mind the following:

Blow the Stench Away

The most important aspect of a conventional outhouse is finding the right location for it, so it does not interfere with other aspects of your home. First off, there is no amount of sawdust, topsoil, or other material that can completely eliminate the smell of the outhouse, especially as it fills up.

Finding a good location that is downwind from your home and outdoor areas is a good start in determining a suitable location. It will also need to be covered, and the outhouse moved at some point in time when the hole fills.

Down the Hill

Although there are many outhouse designs that minimize waste runoff, you do not want to take any risk with locating your outhouse above your home and water supply. Find a good place that is significantly downhill; that way, any runoff will not affect water quality or the health of your living and recreational spaces.

The Outhouse Does Not Need to be Ugly

Most people equate an outhouse with some rickety old shack with a couple of holes cut into it. They think of an outhouse as being a structure that is built on the idea of bare necessity, nothing more.

This does not need to be the case with your off-grid outhouse, as modern-day designs can make the outhouse pleasing to the eye, which will invite more usage. Some outhouses are built with water collection that allows a place to wash your hands and are painted and decorated to be cute and cozy. It doesn't need to be an awful experience to use the outhouse.

Water Hookup?

If the goal of your outhouse is to maximize its usage, then having a water hookup to the outhouse for a sink to wash your hands is a crucial component. There is a wide range of portable hand washing stations that are designed for outdoor food vendors that can also be utilized for servicing an outhouse. For those looking to save money, the construction of a hot water sink is easier than you may think.

Ultimately, an outhouse can play a significant role in your way of life. For those choosing an off-grid home in a more populated area, an outhouse may not be the ideal solution. However, for those with plenty of acreages to spare and wide-open spaces free from outside influence, an outhouse is a simple and inexpensive way to reduce the strain on your indoor plumbing and can provide an enriching experience for reducing your overall environmental footprint.

Composting Toilet

A composting toilet is also referred to as a dry toilet. This means that a water connection is not necessary, and the primary focus of the toilet is to dry the contents and begin the natural process of biodegradation that happens when organic matter is broken down to dirt once again.

There are many types of composting toilets that you can choose from. Some require electricity, while others are completely self-contained for off-grid purposes.

Systemic composting

Depending on how technical you want to get with your bathroom waste, you can set up a fairly sophisticated system to fully compost your waste into non-hazardous, usable compost using the bin method. This method involves 2 bins using various techniques to divert (or not) urine from the mix.

There are many resources out there to delve into the science of human waste composting, and this method will allow you to avoid having to move your outhouse from place to place over the years. Additionally, a composting toilet can be used in this manner for an indoor toilet, since it will need to be emptied frequently, which will mitigate odors.

Self-composting toilet

It is not glamorous, but if you are looking to significantly reduce your water usage with efficient bathroom design for your toilet, going the route of a self-composting toilet is the route to take.

First, it is important to refute some of the myths that go along with self-composting toilets. These can easily detract you from the idea even when you do not have sufficient information to fully analyze the pros and cons.

Composting Toilets Do Not Need to Be Outhouses

As noted before, if you are taking on the composting challenge yourself, you can install a composting toilet just about anywhere. Since the removal of waste will be frequent, they can even be installed inside, although they are far from conventional and may emit unpleasant odors from time to time.

If your off-grid home will be subject to cold weather, the outdoor toilet may not be attractive to you, especially in the winter months. Luckily, the self-composting toilet was designed specifically to be installed inside as they emit virtually no odor, and the material removed will be fully composted and omit little to no odor whatsoever. There is also a wide range of designs to choose from.

Although these toilets run up to 4 times the price of a conventional toilet, the savings on water usage will make up the difference in cost in the matter of a few years. In analyzing the feasibility of an indoor self-composting toilet, there are several things you need to keep in mind:

1. Regular maintenance: self-composting toilets require that you empty them on a regular basis. It is recommended that the urine tray be emptied daily and that the entire storage toilet be emptied after a maximum of 90 uses.

2. Access to Electricity: In order to ventilate and aerate the self-composting toilet, the best designs require that the toilet have access to a power source. The power source will serve the rotator in the toilet, which turns over the waste to mix it with the peat moss that is part of the composting process.

3. A Willingness to Get Dirty: A self-composting toilet is only effective if the owner is willing to utilize the compost when it is time to empty the holding tank. Yes, cleaning out a tank of feces does not sound too appealing; however, what may be even less appealing is the amount of water you are wasting on flushing these feces into a holding tank that needs to be regularly maintained.

By cutting down on what you put in your septic tank, you are extending its life and ultimately saving yourself thousands of dollars in maintenance costs. The cost-benefit analysis will be left for the individual off-grid homeowner to conduct. Still, it is a real consideration when weighing what type of relationship you need to have with your toilet.

Conventional Toilet

Conventional toilets have been around since 1952 when Sir John Harrington invented the first water closet that consisted of a raised cistern and a downpipe that would flush the waste out of the residence. Since that time, the technology of toilets has seen some adjustments but has mostly run on the same premises of using fresh water to flush the waste down a pipe.

Luckily, with the growing concern of freshwater supply, companies have seen an increased interest in reducing the water usage of conventional toilets and have developed toilets to meet the demand of consumers to reduce their water usage through the flushing of a toilet. The average person flushes over 5,000 gallons of water per year. That is a lot of perfectly good water that is essentially wasted.

Low flow

There is no reason now to go with any type of conventional toilet that is not low flow. Since 1994, every toilet manufactured was required to use a maximum of 1.6 gallons of water per flush. Many companies have now lowered this per-flush water usage to as little as 1.2 gallons.

A great way to find the right low flow toilet for your off-grid home is to have a side-by-side comparison of what is on the market today. Only through this research can you find the right toilet to fit your budget and needs.

Shower, Tub or Both?

This book is not meant to weigh in on personal hygiene habits. However, this book is meant to stimulate ideas on how you can achieve proper hygiene in the most efficient manner possible while saving valuable resources. With water savings being the general theme of analyzing off-grid bathrooms, the discussion must inevitably turn from the toilet to the shower.

Space is the number one consideration of whether you should have a shower stall or bathtub. Showers can be efficiently designed to take up very little space. One of the best ways to research the right shower/tub combination for small bathrooms is to look for design ideas for showers in tiny houses.

A consideration for those who enjoy a soak might be a portable Japanese soaking tub that allows you to soak your bones without taking a lot of space or utilize a lot of water either. Considerations should be given to the type of water source you have access to. If you are relying on rainwater collection, you may not wish to waste that water on a bathtub.

Why a Shower Stall Makes Sense

Tiny house designs are meant to maximize every square foot of space, and the shower or bathtub is no different from the rest of the house. Although the size of the shower may ensure that there is very little room to move about, this does not mean that the shower design itself has to skimp on style. Some great ideas for tiny showers that look stylish and are quite effective can be found by visiting https://www.thespruce.com/tiny-showers-4156387.

Beyond the shower design itself, the water production of the showerhead can also be maximized for efficiency by finding the right design that minimizes water usage while also not sacrificing water pressure. One of the major misconceptions about shower heads is that the higher the pressure, the more water the head uses. This is not true, as it is the air generated by the showerhead that creates the pressure, not the amount of water coming through it.

High-pressure shower heads can make up for low water pressure. This is especially important for off-grid homes that are tapped into freshwater springs that struggle to produce the water necessary to generate high water pressure throughout the home's plumbing.

As with all parts of the home, do not commit to purchasing a showerhead until you have compared it with its competition. What you are looking for is a mixture of pressure with the lowest amount of water usage possible. A great side-by-side comparison of these types of showerheads can be found at https://www.beyondshower.com/.

Outdoor Showers

Outdoor showers are another great way to reduce the strain on your septic while providing an enriching experience for its users. There is nothing as exhilarating as a shower outside in the early morning chill. When contemplating about an outdoor shower, there are two schools of thought when it comes to design.

The Permanent Outdoor Shower

If you have the resources and space, an outdoor shower hooked to the plumbing will allow you to utilize the outdoor season for at least three seasons out of the year, depending on your location. These designs can be simple backyard shower heads, or they can take on a more glamorous approach. Remember that being off-the-grid doesn't mean that you've got to rough it.

The major components of the outdoor shower are the showerhead and sufficient drainage to move the water away from the house, allowing it to be absorbed into the earth naturally. You should use an environmentally friendly soap and shampoo if you are going to let this soapy water run back into your soil and your groundwater. We'll cover that in more detail below.

Camping/Portable Outdoor Showers

If you are looking for something a little more primitive but also effective, a camping/outdoor shower can allow you to use any canopy of trees as a shower curtain and any flat piece of ground as your shower stall. Although these portable showers can get the job done, they also require more initiative from the user than if they are using a permanent outdoor shower.

The goal always is to facilitate regular use of the outdoor shower to save strain on your infrastructure. This cost/benefit analysis should be considered thoroughly before you determine what type of outdoor shower will best meet you and your family's needs while also passing on the best possible benefit it can by the facilitation of regular use.

Outdoor Showers Need Biodegradable Soap

Regardless of the outdoor shower chosen, the soap you use is the most important part of the process to ensure you are not needlessly contaminating groundwater with needless chemicals. Finding an all-natural soap that is considered safe for outdoor use is essential. A list of some of the best soaps to use can be located at https://thedyrt.com/magazine/gear/.

Saving Water with a Bathtub

There is little way around it. If you enjoy a good bath, you are going to need to utilize more square footage to accommodate this luxury. Although the required square footage may pose an obstacle, the utilization of a bathtub has other efficiency benefits; number one being that the water you use in the bath can be recycled for other uses besides filing up your gray water septic tank.

On average, baths use 36 gallons of water. This is nearly twice the amount of water that is used in a 10-minute shower. This water, although contaminated with your bacteria and dirt at the end, can be recycled to perform many other tasks that require water; number one is flushing the toilet. With one bath, you have generated enough water for flushing your toilet upwards of 18 times if you use a low-flow toilet or 7 times if you use a conventional toilet.

Completing the Water Saving Project with the Right Sink

A sink is meant to perform a very straightforward task, which is to provide water for the hands to manipulate. It is not meant to be fancy; it is not meant to instill awe from guests, rather it serves a simple purpose. With simplicity in mind, you can forge a great relationship with your sink by ensuring that it performs what it needs to, while ensuring that both space and water used is minimized.

Small is Best

As an off-grid homeowner, you have chosen a route of getting the most out of your home without the need for excessive frills. Choosing a space-efficient sink is an easy way to continue this theme, and with a little research, you can find a sink that is not only space-efficient but also effective in performing the duties it is required to perform.

Wall-Mounted Sink

The most economic sink on the market today for those looking to save space is the wall-mounted sink. Easy to install to any wall studs and it takes up as little as 2 square feet of space. These sinks can be installed anywhere in a bathroom to facilitate efficient use. Do not be fooled though, the high-power faucet can deliver as much water pressure as you need.

Vessel Above-Counter Sink

If you have installed a vanity for storage and working space and want to double the use of this space to include sink installation, the vessel above-the-counter sink is a great option. A simple bowl design with a faucet is installed on top of the vanity and takes up less than 4 square feet of counter space.

Corner Wall Mounted Sink

By far the most space-efficient of all sinks, the corner wall mounted sink can be signed for right or left-handed users and can be installed in what would otherwise be considered dead space in the corner area of a bathroom. It may not be extravagant, but it serves the purpose and allows for most of the remaining bathroom space to be utilized for other, more important aspects of the bathroom.

CHAPTER 10: Deciding on a Power System

Depending on geographic location and the position of your land, there are various systems and combinations of systems that can give you your basic power needs and allow you to operate completely off-grid. These all require a significant investment to start, but eventually, depending on how you finance them, allow for free electricity for many years.

First-Weigh the Cost Versus the Incentives

Before you begin the process of choosing the right power generator for your off-grid home, it is important for you to understand where the federal and state-level incentives are that can have a significant impact on the system's overall cost.

What Programs Exist to Reduce the Cost?

A good place to start your funding search for grants or low-interest loans is the U.S. Department of Energy. You will find an abundance of information on different types of funding for your green energy project and can even apply for this assistance online.

Keep in mind that this funding can be highly competitive, and much of it is geared towards business development as opposed to personal power generation. However, just completing the application can be a useful exercise in stimulating your creativity to seek out additional sources of funding for your power generation that you may not have known existed before.

Tax Credits

One of the easiest ways to leverage your green power system into savings is through tax credits that can be applied to your project. According to Energystar.gov, tax credits for green energy installation are applied through the following step-down procedure:

- 30% for systems placed in service by 12/31/2019
- 26% for systems placed in service after 12/31/2019 and before 01/01/2021
- 22% for systems placed in service after 12/31/2020 and before 01/01/2022

If your off-grid home is pre-existing (i.e., you are remodeling and not building from scratch), and the home will be your primary residence, you may also be entitled to an additional 10% tax credit for the cost of the equipment up to a maximum of $500.

State Tax Incentives/Rebates

Beyond what is offered through the federal government, most states may also provide incentives to entice homeowners into installing green energy products.

A good place to find your local tax incentives is to visit the state-by-state database which is located at https://www.dsireusa.org/.

Local/Municipal Incentives

Beyond the federal and state incentives, local governments may also offer some incentives. Although these incentives may be smaller than those offered by the federal and state government, they are also less competitive, which can increase the likelihood of you receiving the assistance requested.

Talk to your local zoning or planning board to seek out information on these programs.

Solar

When thinking about going off-grid, the first thing most people think about is solar panels. They are the most common system, the most consistent source of power, and currently, with a growing trend for companies "going solar," there are more and more companies popping up to take care of the design and installation for you at competitive prices.

Solar power arrays consist of a solar panel either installed on a pole, mounted on a roof, the side of a house or solar panels that may be stand-alone or mounted on a roof or other portion of your house depending on the angle of your property in relation to the direction of the sun.

This could seriously affect your choice of homesite should you desire to use your roof for the solar array as opposed to free-standing. There are even photovoltaic "shingles," so the solar array can be discreetly installed into the roof of your home.

The positioning of the panels at the correct angle and direction is key to the amount of power you can convert from the sun. The most effective positioning for solar panels is south or southwest (depending on location), and panels do the best positioning perpendicular to the sun's path.

Some newer, free-standing solar panels are designed to move into the best position throughout the day, so you won't have to worry about repositioning at different times of the year. This is a very beneficial option that works to ensure that you have more hours of direct sunlight throughout the day.

Other equipment you will need involve converting the power from the sun into usable electricity with a solar inverter and a special output meter. These are responsible for monitoring the electric output to the home, which will prevent power surges on sunny days and to help distribute the power evenly.

If your house site is already connected to the grid, you may consider looking into programs that power companies have been adopting to buy back unused power from customers. With this, you could end up making money on your solar panels, or at least offsetting your power bill during the dark months.

However, most people who are truly off-grid use a set of batteries to store the power they collect. There are many types of batteries to choose from, depending on your electricity needs. The batteries will normally be the greatest cost in your solar system, and you should try to get the best batteries that you can afford as they'll last longer and give you better service.

There are several types of batteries to choose from:

- **LEAD ACID** - The electrodes are metallic lead-containing lead oxides that change in composition during charging and discharging.

They are filled with a fluid, which is an electrolyte diluted sulfuric acid. * **AGM batteries** are technically in this grouping, but they are sealed and do not discharge gas like regular lead-acid batteries. This makes them safer and maintenance-free. They last longer as well.

- **LITHIUM** - These have a very long life cycle and can be discharged and recharged lower and higher. These are widely accepted as the best batteries that you can get for your solar system.

- **NICKEL-CADMIUM** - Not good for solar. Very expensive, expensive to dispose of, and only have an efficiency of about 65%, which is far lower than Lithium, and can reach 90% efficiency.

Ultimately, the major consideration in solar is whether you have the right type of land that is conducive to the sun production you need to maximize your solar production. This determination should be made prior to the construction of the home. It should come when you are working on the land to build the proper site. In determining whether solar is a viable option for your building site, here are a few tips in ensuring that you make the right decision.

Watch How the Sun Travels on the Site:

It may seem straightforward, but it is actually a complex task in observing how the sun travels on your parcel of land. In order to most accurately depict the path of the sun, you will need to observe where it hits your parcel during different parts of the day and to mark the areas where the sun hits the strongest.

This can be difficult if your building lot contains significant woodlands, as the sun will often be blocked from striking the ground due to the tree cover.

However, marking the spots where the sun does breakthrough is a great way to find where the sun's power is the strongest.

Keep in mind that the closer to winter, the lower the sun will travel in the sky. This variation between summer and winter will allow you to determine where the sun hits in all seasons, making it easier for you to determine a viable spot to place your solar panels.

A useful resource in charting the sun can be found by reading the following article located at https://www.permaculturenews.org/2015/10/23/.

Making Site Modifications to Facilitate the Sun's Path

Once you have charted the sun and marked it appropriately on your site, the next step is to determine what type of site modifications you will need to complete in order to capture the path of the sun in the most efficient manner. Trees are often the biggest obstacle in the site modification for solar. The biggest decision you will need to make regarding site modification is determining what trees you will need to remove and what impact that removal will have on the overall site plan.

Do I Cut Tree Down or Remove Limbs?

After you have constructed your chart of the sun's path, it will be easier for you to determine exactly what you need to do with the trees that block the sun's access to the ground. Removal of entire trees can be a difficult decision to make, especially if the trees provide good shade to areas of the site that you deem will be used often.

In such cases, where you are weighing the value of the tree with the value of the sun it is blocking, you may be able to negotiate some by only removing certain limbs that have the most impact while maintaining the integrity of the tree.

Pruning a tree's limbs will not only be less expensive and time-consuming, but it may also, in certain instances, have the same impact as if you removed the entire tree when it comes to capturing the sun.

It may be a good idea at this point in the planning to consult with a professional arborist. They will be able to fully analyze the tree and weigh the risks you run in removing limbs as opposed to cutting down the entire tree. They may also be able to access the overall health of the tree in order to estimate whether the tree poses dangers that require it to be taken down completely or if it has a lot of years of healthy growth that can sustain the pruning of it while still maintaining its overall health.

Does the Ground Need to Be Modified to Capture More Sun?

Another consideration in determining the viability of a solar site is the ground contours that make up the site. If you are operating on a flat site, this question is easy to answer. However, if your site is located in a hillier landscape, you may need to consider how these hills may play a role in the overall viability of the solar system.

Moving the earth is expensive. Excavating companies can often charge well over $100 per hour and flattening or modifying hillsides can be ripe with potential impediments. If your plan is to flatten a rise on the site, and you run into a ledge while doing so, you either have to blast through it or move your proposed site for solar to a different location.

Ensuring Your Site Plan Does not Conflict with Other Infrastructure

Although it may appear that you have found an excellent site for your solar, if it conflicts with your water, sewer, or electric, you may have to modify your plans to ensure that one part of your infrastructure does not conflict with another.

This concern makes it important for you to plan all aspects of your infrastructure prior to any construction. This will ensure that a solid plan has been put into place to ensure a cooperative approach between all aspects of the infrastructure before breaking ground.

Wind

Wind power is available for certain off-grid homes where it is determined that the land can harness enough of the natural wind to turn it into power. Commonly, this is completed by the installation of wind turbines. Wind turbines use the natural power of the wind to generate kinetic energy. This energy runs through an internal generator that, in turn, converts the wind into clean energy.

The technology behind wind power has constantly evolved since its invention in 1988. The turbines have gone through significant modifications, focusing on the aerodynamics of the turbines that create more energy with less size.

Much has been reported about the use of wind as a supplemental source of power. Small wind turbines have been installed in a wide range of areas to serve both large- and small-scale power generation.

The appealing nature of wind turbines, however, has also come with quite a bit of controversy. Opponents of wide-scale wind power have complained that the wind turbines are noisy, ruin the beauty of natural ridgelines, and can have a negative impact on native bird populations. These claims are false.

It has also recently been discovered that painting one of the propellers of the wind generator can reduce bird fatalities to almost zero. The smaller windmills should not be attached to your cabin because doing so will be noisy as they vibrate in the wind, and this will be exacerbated by traveling through the home. Move the generator to a space away from the home, on a pole, and you won't hear it or feel it.

On the flip side, proponents of wind power have argued that wind is one of the most efficient ways to generate power, and it is available to a wide range of municipalities, businesses, and individuals at a modest cost.

In some instances, wind can be the primary source of power for a residence or business, while in others, it can drastically reduce your overall dependency on more conventional power generation. It depends on where you live. Most wind generators need to have at a minimum, 7 mile-per-hour winds to generate any power.

Where they seem to have the most benefit is in hybrid power systems that utilize a mixture of solar and wind, ensuring that no matter what the weather is like, power is being generated. Both small and large systems can be very effective for a multitude of varying applications.

To evaluate the feasibility of wind as a power generator on your off-grid home, you should begin the process by researching the following.

What Role Do I Want Wind Power to Play in Power Generation?

There are two ways to evaluate the power usage required in wind generation. Do you want it to supplement your power generation with other forms of clean energy such as solar or geothermal? Or are you looking for wind to be the primary power generator of your home?

Some may say that you need to look at your building site first to see if wind power is even feasible before you decide what role wind will play. However, determining the viability of the site can be an expensive proposition.

Instead, first look to the anticipated goal and then work backward to see if the goal is achievable by the land you have purchased. This will ensure that you do not jump the gun on committing to a wind system that, although feasible from a building standpoint, may not ultimately fit your goals and budget.

Matching Cost with Power Output

The cost of a wind turbine is based on the expected power it will generate. According to the American Wind Energy Association (AWEA), even a small wind turbine can cost in the neighborhood of $3,000-$5,000 for every kilowatt of power it produces.

Most homeowners using a wind turbine as their primary source of electricity install between 5 to 15 kW of wind power capacity, meaning they can expect to pay between $15,000 and $75,000 for their small wind turbine project.

Determining Benefits Versus Negatives

Wind power is more discriminate in where it can generate power. If there is not enough wind to turn the turbines, then it is useless. This is why it is so important that you carefully study the locations that might be available before committing to the project if you plan to select wind power for your off-grid home.

What About Zoning Regulations?

Even if your home is suitable for a wind turbine, the town in which your home will be located may have regulations that limit or even eliminate the possibility of installing a wind turbine in the desired area.

There is nothing more inefficient than paying for a plan and then finding out that the local government will not permit its construction due to zoning laws. In general, there are far more restrictions on wind turbines as opposed to solar due to the potential intrusion the turbines may have on wildlife and other residents.

In many towns, a permit for a wind turbine, no matter the size, is required prior to construction. Often you will need to accompany this permit application with a site plan along with the specifications of the intended turbine. This will often require a hearing in front of an elected zoning board where those that may be affected by the turbine may voice objections to the proposal.

Never assume that your plan will be approved simply because it is an attempt to become greener in your energy production. Although this is certainly a noble cause, there is much at play when you are talking about installing a large tower that generates noise, impacts ridgelines or viewpoints, and may have an impact on natural habitat such as bird populations.

Ensure that you know the process, and if confusing, you ought to have an attorney and/or wind turbine professional ready to testify as to the impact the windmill will have. Only through this careful presentation will you be able to maximize your chances of fending off potential challenges.

To prepare you for the zoning hearing, be sure to look into the following:

- Reach out to the local zoning board, building inspector, or other similar government officials to seek out the information you need to file an application.

- Visit the Permitting and Zoning Resource Center of energy.gov.

- Visit Distributed Wind Energy Zoning and Permitting: A Toolkit for Local Governments.

As with other aspects of the building process, you can save a substantial amount of money by doing your own leg work first before you seek the assistance of professionals.

Wind Feasibility Study

If wind power is going to be your primary generator of electricity, then it may be worth conducting a wind feasibility study before beginning construction. Experts are trained to evaluate the landscape of a proposed windmill and determine the areas where the most power can be generated.

Although this study may cost several thousands of dollars to complete, the peace of mind you have knowing that your investment will be maximized is well worth the start-up cost.

Once a proposed site has been found on your land, the next step in the process is to figure out how this site coincides with other aspects of your home. There are a substantial number of factors that you will need to consider in determining whether the proposed site will fit in with the overall goals of your home.

Size of Turbine

The size of a residential turbine can range from 400 watts to 100 kW depending on the amount of power you wish to generate. The major issues that you must calculate in finding the right sized turbine for your home are the anticipated energy needs along with the estimated wind speed of your site.

In general, the higher the wind speed, the more power can be generated. If you are looking for a majority or all of your power to be generated by the wind turbine, you will need to correlate the anticipated power generation required with the wind speed estimates.

This formula will give you a rough idea of the sized turbine you will need and how this requirement matches your goals, as well as the limitations that you may face as a result of zoning regulations.

The complicated nature of determining an appropriate wind turbine size makes the wind feasibility study even more important. With all aspects of your building process, you never want to install more than you need.

However, what may be even more inefficient is installing less than what you need. This re-emphasizes the importance of taking a cautious and well thought out approach before you commit the financial resources to the project.

Is the Site Really Worth It?

Even if you have an ideal site for a wind turbine that will produce large quantities of energy, you must still ask yourself the question of whether or not the installation of the wind turbine, given all of its characteristics, is really worth it when compared to other, potentially less intrusive manners of power generation.

There has been much debate about the value of wind turbines on ridgelines, especially those within the view of populous areas. It has been argued that the negative impact of the deterioration of these ridgelines outweighs the benefit of green energy production.

Although your personal windmill will be far less intrusive than those large wind farms you see across the country, the impact may be just as drastic for you and your neighbors if the windmill takes away an ideal natural spot that would otherwise be enjoyed for outdoor activities.

Beyond the aesthetic impact of a wind turbine, you must also weigh the impact the turbine will have on other important aspects of your home. Turbines require land clearing, maintenance, and it take up valuable air space.

Not only will this have an impact on the ground surrounding the turbine, it will also have an impact on the natural habitat. If granted, this impact will be far less dramatic than that of large-scale wind turbines, but the localized effect it will have on your home site may be just as substantial.

CHAPTER 11: Heat Sources - Options

There has been no better time for an off-grid heating system than now. As reliance on fossil fuels continues to decline and technology continues to evolve, the options for heating your home are in abundance.

With the plentiful options, however, also comes difficult decisions, especially for those who live in colder climates. What you need in your heating system is a combination of efficiency and practicality.

You do not want to have more heat than you need, but also do not want to run the risk of having less heat than what you require. When trying to facilitate the right decision for your off-grid home, it's important to analyze each potential heat source and how this interacts with its natural environment.

Wood Heat - The Age-Old Classic

Wood heat has been around since harnessing fire was first discovered 2 million years ago. Although the harnessing of wood heat has changed quite a bit since that time, the premises remain the same; burning dry wood equals consistent heat.

Simple, right? Not quite. Although burning wood has always been considered folksy and enjoyable when it is not a primary heat source, relying on wood to heat your off-grid home is far more complicated.

Finding the Source

The first step in determining whether wood heat makes sense for your home is deciding where this wood is coming from. Do you intend to harvest the wood on your own, or do you intend to have a third party deliver the wood to your home? This answer alone can make a big difference in weighing the feasibility as your primary heat source.

Do It Yourself? Are You Sure You Can?

It sounds romantic, doesn't it? Out in the woods on your own, armed with a chainsaw, cutting your own trees to provide a basic necessity for you and your family. As attractive as this may sound, let's get into the details before signing off on this romance novel.

What wood are you cutting?

Yes, it is true that most, if not all wood, burns eventually. However, each type of wood burns differently. Softwood trees, such as pine, cedar, spruce, larch, and fir, retain their leaves throughout the year and are known to grow faster than hardwoods.

Softwoods are also notorious for burning fast and dirty. This means that should you choose to fill your woodstove primarily with softwoods, you will need to cut more and will need to clean your chimney far more often.

If you have more hardwoods such as oak or maple on your land, count yourself fortunate, as these woods will burn cleaner and longer than softwoods.

How much wood do you need?

Determining the amount of wood or cords required to heat your home can be a complicated calculation. The primary factors in determining the amount of wood are first to understand how efficient your home is.

If the home is a new construction with a focus on energy efficiency, depending on your location, it may require as little as four cords of wood to heat a 2,000 square foot home for the entire year. However, if the home is older, draftier, and has less insulation, it may take upwards of twice as much wood.

How quickly can I burn wood that has been cut?

Wood needs to be dried before you use it on your stove. It is often a good practice to let it dry at least three months before burning it, especially if the wood is exposed to the elements.

If the wood is covered, you may be able to reduce the dry time by 33%. What is important to remember is that you should never try to burn wood right after it is harvested, as it can cause substantial issues not only regarding efficiency but also with regards to stove maintenance.

After You Have Committed to Wood, Choose a Stove

There are two schools of thought when it comes to finding the right wood stove to heat your home. The first is to have a centralized furnace located in a basement that distributes the heat generated through a series of ducts throughout the home. This can be the most efficient way to burn wood, but requires a substantial amount of installation work.

The second school is to install a series of smaller wood stoves in areas that are heavily used. These stoves will heat specific rooms, and if vented correctly, the heat will also travel upwards to bedrooms or other areas that do not have a stove in them.

In either case, the key to properly distribute the heat is to ensure that there is a proper chimney installed that will vent the smoke from the burning wood out of the house while also ensuring that a maximum amount of the heat travels throughout the house.

Stove Choices

There is a wide range of wood stoves on the market today. The market for ambiance along with cheap heat production, has brought many consumers back to the roots of wood heating by reinventing an age-old pastime. As a result, quality wood stoves remain in high demand.

For your heating project, you will need to determine how each stove meets the heating requirements of the space it occupies. For basement furnaces, the key is to find a stove that matches the required BTUs to heat the entire home. For small homes, the trick is to find a stove that won't burn too hot and make it so hot that it's intolerable indoors.

Generally speaking, it takes approximately 3,000 BTUs to heat 100 square feet of living space. Luckily wood furnaces are designed to burn upwards of 160,000 BTUs, which should, if properly vented, can take a significant bite out of your heating requirements each year.

For localized stoves, the focus again is on BTU production, but this must also be correlated with the heat requirements for each stove. Thought must also be given to whether the stove will have multiple uses, such as doubling as a cookstove. Regardless of the need, there are several major stoves that are worth considering.

Open Fireplace

By far the most iconic of the localized heat production methods, but also the most inefficient and, for the sake of transparency, the most wasteful. The open fireplace requires a chimney to vent and, due to the openness of its design, will heat very little beyond the immediate area surrounding the fireplace.

If you are looking for a fire to cozy up next to and read a book, this is a great design but if you are looking for something to heat your home, stay as far away from the open fireplace as possible.

There are many other far more efficient models of wood-burning stoves, and we will explore them all below. Ensure that your stove is rated safe and that you have it professionally installed unless you know very well how to do so.

Improper installation can result in burning your home to the ground, and it happens far too often. You have to ensure that where the stovepipe passes through to the wall to vent is correctly insulated, as this is essential. The wall can get so hot that it ignites if the stove pipe isn't properly vented and insulated.

Potbelly Stove

Considered one of the most iconic of all the wood stoves, a potbelly stove gets its name from its wide midriff that is designed to hold a significant amount of fuel, which allows it to burn at extremely high heat.

Some of the newer potbelly stoves have been rated at around 200,000 BTUs, which turns this simple design into a heat-producing machine. A potbelly stove can also double as a cooktop, as its flat heat allows you to heat water or cook anything that you could also use a conventional burner for.

The potbelly stove could burn coal or wood but is used with wood today. Ensure that burning wood is allowed where you live, and if you're on wheels, this is very important to check into before lighting up your heat source.

Traditional Cookstove

These stoves have been designed to last, as they have been popular in both on and off-grid homes for over a hundred years.

The cookstove is the ultimate hybrid, designed to heat a kitchen as well as provide a primary cooking source. These stoves often contain both a burner top and an oven that can be used to bake.

The one challenge with cookstoves is that the firewood needed to fuel these stoves cannot be large; it needs to be cut down to smaller pieces, which will result in a demand to feed the stove more often than other stoves.

Although the fire may need to be fed more often, if you are merely looking to maintain a modest temperature, the cookstove design is perfect for maintaining a warm bed of coals that keep a consistent temperature for both cooking and heating.

Proper venting is essential with cookstoves as they can generate a lot of smoke. Ensuring there is a direct linear to the chimney will ensure the smoke feeds outside while also capturing the heat that can be transferred to upstairs rooms for further heating efficiency.

Masonry Stove

Masonry stoves are designed like potbelly stoves. Their focus is to burn fast and hot. This results in a cleaner burn than from stoves that focus more on coal preservation (i.e., a cookstove).

Often referred to by its German name, the *Kachelofen stove*, this design is based on a complex series of heat-exchange passages that harness the fire's gasses. This design allows for the heat to be consistently and slowly circulated, which is great for maintaining consistent temperatures for long periods.

Modern Day Woodstove

The EPA became increasingly concerned with the emissions from wood stoves in the late 1980s. As a result, new technology focused on a cleaner-burning wood stove. Phrases such as catalytic and noncatalytic have been used to describe these new designs.

Regardless of whether you chose a catalytic or non-catalytic design, the goal of the stove remains the same; to fully combust the wood fuel and eliminate emissions that cause CO_2 from being emitted into the air. Not only are these stoves better for the environment, they also burn more efficiently than more traditional stoves.

Wood Pellet Stoves

For those who enjoy the efficiency of a wood stove but do not want to deal with the hassle of firewood, a wood pellet stove may be an excellent alternative. As is the case with traditional wood stoves, pellet stoves have continued to evolve with new models designed to provide heat for an entire home or focus solely on heating one space.

The average home will require the burning of 2-3 tons of pellets per year to heat their home. At an average cost of $250 per ton, heating with pellets can be a cost-effective way to heat your home while avoiding much of the labor that is required with firewood.

Another major appeal for pellets over firewood is the venting requirement. Customarily, when burning firewood, you are required to hook the stove up to the chimney. With efficiency and safety in mind, your chimney would also require a liner to be installed in the chimney.

It is also important for the chimney to be cleaned yearly to ensure that the carbon buildup, or soot as it is commonly referred to, does not build up in the chimney. This reduces the risk of fire.

With pellet stoves, they are designed to be vented out the wall with its only metal pipe and are not required to be hooked into your chimney. This opens up the use of the pellet stove for areas not directly connected to the chimney, which can allow you to efficiently heat areas that are often considered cold spots in a home when burning with wood.

Now the Negative

The major negatives for wood stove heating, beyond the requirement of securing all the wood, is the inconsistency of how the heat is applied to the house. It is easy, if you do not plan appropriately, for there to be cold and hot spots throughout the house.

These irregularities are largely because the heat will travel, literally, as the wind blows. This means that if you have a drafty home and a cross breeze, that the heat can be transferred in an inconsistent manner and can, in fact, heat areas that it was not intended to heat while leaving other areas colder than desired.

There are some ways to combat the inconsistency issue.

- There are specially designed fans that are used for wood stoves that will force the hot air to circulate throughout the room as opposed to remaining stagnant. These fans can be installed at the top of the stove, where a majority of the heat escapes and can then be blown outwardly to reach more areas of the home.

- Open spaces: If it is your intent to heat with wood before the house is built, one of the best ways to ensure that wood heat will be effective is to design your home with a lot of open space. Wood heat can get trapped or fenced off if there are a lot of walls separated for living space. By removing as many barriers as you can from your heat source, you are allowing the heat to travel freely throughout the home, which will help immensely in eliminating cold spots.

Never Stop Looking to Close Up Outdoor Leaks

As is the case with all heating sources, but especially with wood heat, the more insulated you are from the outdoors, the better and more consistent the wood will heat the home.

Even in new construction, there are ways to increase overall efficiency that can be as easy as plugging small holes, installing door, inserts that seal off the space between the bottom of the door and the threshold. This means ensuring that all windows have storm windows and that they are sealed tightly during the winter months. This is also part of shoring up the leaks.

Geothermal Heating and Cooling

Take note!

Before you start to contemplate on a geothermal system for your off-grid home, keep in mind that these systems are customarily designed to produce heating and cooling only.

Although the savings on heating costs can be upwards of 70-80% over conventional heating sources such as oil or propane, you will still need to have a separate power generator beyond what geothermal can provide.

Geothermal heating and cooling systems for homes have become increasingly popular for residential construction as the technology in these systems have evolved and become more affordable. In general, there are three different types of geothermal systems that can be used for residential construction.

Vertical closed-loop systems

A U-shaped design, the vertical closed-loop system continuously circulates fluid through a high-density polyethylene piping that allows either cooling or heating to be circulated from the ground into the home.

The issue with these systems is that you are generally required to dig at least 300 feet for these systems to work properly. The cost to install these systems is usually calculated by the foot, which will equate to a significant up-front cost.

Horizontal closed-loop systems

The horizontal closed-loop systems generate heating and cooling in the same manner as vertical systems, except that the pipe layout runs the liquid back and forth underground.

The installation of horizontal systems requires the digging of trenches as opposed to a well, which can be more efficient in initial installation costs over the vertical design.

The downside to horizontal systems is that they require a large amount of ground space. If your off-grid home is on a small plot of land, you should cross this potential design off your list immediately, as the land you own will not be able to properly facilitate the horizontal design.

Open-loop systems

An open-loop system utilized groundwater is pumped directly from a water supply well, which is customarily 75 to 100 feet deep. To generate heat or cooling, the water is pumped out of the first well. After the heat exchange is carried out, the water is injected into the second well.

Open-loop systems are by far the most cost-effective out of all the designs and can be the most efficient. However, in order to use an open looped system, you must have an abundance of groundwater.

If there is any question as to this requirement, especially with the needs dictated by your freshwater supply for the home, an open-loop system may not be the best choice.

Geothermal heating systems can be a great way to efficiently heat your home. However, there are many requirements beyond the system itself that are required that take a lot of specialized planning.

As is the case with most systems, you should first determine the feasibility of the system before committing to it. The extra consultation time can save you a lot of money in the long run.

Chapter 12: Putting It All Together

Your off-grid home can be whatever you want it to be. The things that make it your home, after all, are the unique touches that you incorporate into the design.

The blood, sweat, and tears that you invest during the building process will give you instant equity and generate a sense of pride you've never felt before.

You are in the driver's seat. The plan, the design, the remoteness, the type of heating, method of power generation, and just how off-grid you are is completely up to you. Buy land or lease. Permanently affix your home to land or build it on wheels and travel where the road takes you.

What makes your house a home will be the memories you create in it, and surrounding yourself with the people and possessions that are the most important to you will ensure that those moments you create will be special and unique.

Your budget, now that you understand how to put it together is within your ability to control. We've shown you the tools and given you the information to put it all together, create your checklist, and build that home.

You can build it from new materials or go the upcycled route. Totally your call. No matter what you choose to do, just take it one step at a time, and the next thing you know, you'll be moving into your own house, customized just for you.

The draw of off-grid living is living sustainably while reducing your carbon footprint. The allure is also about challenging oneself to see how far you can escape from the things that have made our species lazy and ruined the environment.

Become the steward of the earth that you've always wanted to be and build your off-grid castle to raise your children in, teaching them that life isn't about what we own in our lives but instead, *what we do with our lives.*

www.ingramcontent.com/pod-product-compliance
Ingram Content Group UK Ltd.
Pitfield, Milton Keynes, MK11 3LW, UK
UKHW051259180426
11947UKWH00020B/1803